Ultimate Guide Crafting Delicious Soft Pretzels

Maariya I. Rocha

Ultimate Guide Crafting Delicious Soft Pretzels : Mastering the Art of Creating Irresistible Soft Pretzels at Home

Funny helpful tips:

Maintain a culture of collaboration; teamwork often leads to better results.

Stay connected with developments in gene editing; technologies like CRISPR are paving the way for medical breakthroughs.

Introduction

This book offers a tantalizing array of pretzel recipes to satisfy every craving and occasion. From classic soft pretzels to innovative flavor combinations, this cookbook has something for everyone. Whether you're craving something sweet, savory, or cheesy, you'll find the perfect pretzel recipe to tantalize your taste buds.

For those with a sweet tooth, options like Caramel Pretzel Bites, Nutella Pretzel Bites, and Cinnamon Sugar Pretzels offer irresistible treats that are perfect for dessert or snacking. These indulgent creations combine the salty crunch of pretzels with the rich sweetness of caramel, chocolate, and cinnamon for a truly decadent experience.

Savory options abound as well, with recipes like Cheesy Jalapeno Pretzel Bites, Philly Cheesesteak Pretzels, and Cheeseburger Pretzels offering a satisfyingly savory twist on the classic pretzel. These recipes are perfect for game day snacks, casual gatherings, or anytime you're craving something hearty and satisfying.

For those looking to get creative in the kitchen, the cookbook also includes recipes for innovative flavor combinations like Olive and Garlic Pretzels, Parmesan Crusted Soft Pretzels, and Tomato & Cheese Pretzels. These unique recipes showcase the versatility of pretzels and offer a delicious way to experiment with different flavors and ingredients.

No matter which recipe you choose, each one is accompanied by clear and easy-to-follow instructions, making it simple to recreate these delicious treats at home. With this book in hand, you'll be well-equipped to impress family and friends with your homemade pretzel creations. So roll up your sleeves, preheat the oven, and get ready to bake up a batch of delicious pretzels that are sure to delight your taste buds.

Contents

1. Caramel Pretzel Bites

Soft, lush bread with a gooey caramel center? Sign us up!

Makes: 12 servings

Prep: 2 ½ hrs.

Cook: 10 mins

Ingredients:

- 1 package active dry yeast
- 1 cup warm water
- 1 tbsp. brown sugar
- 3 ¼ cups bread flour
- ½ cup cold milk
- 2 tbsp. unsalted butter, cut into 1 inch pieces, at room temperature, plus more for greasing

- 2 tsp salt
- 1 ½ cups store bought caramel sauce

Directions:

Preheat oven to 500 F.

Into a stand mixer, add in the warm water. Sprinkle on the yeast

Add in the brown sugar. Mix thoroughly and allow to bloom until foamy. This should take about 5 minutes.

Add in the flour, butter, salt, and continue stirring. On low speed, begin kneading the dough for a minute or until it forms a smooth ball. Continue kneading until the dough become pliant – about 5 minutes.

In a lightly greased bowl, place dough and cover with saran wrap. Set away to rise in a warm area for 90 minutes, until double.

Place dough on a floured counter and divide into 12 equal portions.

Roll each piece into a rectangle. Place about 2 tbsp. of caramel sauce in the center.

Pull the two edges of the dough together and pinch to cover. Ensure the caramel is completely covered and set onto a baking tray.

Repeat with the rest of the dough. Place dough pieces 2 inches apart.

Allow to rise for 30 more minutes.

Coat with a quick egg wash before baking for 8-10 minutes until crispy and golden brown.

2. Basic Soft Pretzels

This is a quick and easy pretzel recipe, perfect for evening snack or a late night delight!

Makes: 8 servings

Prep: 2 hrs. 10 mins

Cook: 10 mins

Ingredients:

- 1 package active dry yeast
- 1 cup warm water
- 1 tbsp. brown sugar
- 3 ¼ cups bread flour

- 2 tbsp. unsalted butter, cut into 1 inch pieces, at room temperature, plus more for greasing
- 2 tsp salt

Directions:

Preheat oven to 500 F.

Into a stand mixer, add in the warm water. Sprinkle on the yeast.

Add in the brown sugar. Mix thoroughly and allow to bloom until foamy. This should take about 5 minutes.

Add in the flour, butter, salt, and continue stirring. On low speed, begin kneading the dough for a minute or until it forms a smooth ball. Continue kneading until the dough become pliant – about 5 minutes.

In a lightly greased bowl, place dough and cover with saran wrap. Set away to rise in a warm area for 90 minutes, until double.

Divide into 8 portions and roll out into desired shape – knots, buns, or sticks.

Arrange on 2 lined baking trays about 2 inches apart.

Allow to rise for 30 more minutes.

Coat with a quick egg wash before baking for 8-10 minutes until crispy and golden brown!

3. Whole Wheat Pretzels

Want a healthier option? Try this whole wheat pretzel recipe instead!

Makes: 8 servings

Prep: 2 hrs. 10 mins

Cook: 10 mins

Ingredients:

- 1 package active dry yeast
- 1 cup warm water
- 1 tbsp. brown sugar
- 2 cups bread flour
- 1 ¼ cup whole wheat flour
- 2 tbsp. unsalted butter, cut into 1 inch pieces, at room temperature, plus more for greasing

- 2 tsp salt

Directions:

Preheat oven to 500 F.

Into a stand mixer, add in the warm water. Sprinkle on the yeast

Add in the brown sugar. Mix thoroughly and allow to bloom until foamy. This should take about 5 minutes.

Add in the flours, butter, salt, and continue stirring. On low speed, begin kneading the dough for a minute or until it forms a smooth ball. Continue kneading until the dough become pliant – about 5 minutes.

In a lightly greased bowl, place dough and cover with saran wrap. Set away to rise in a warm area for 90 minutes, until double.

Divide into 8 portions and roll out into desired shape – knots, buns, or sticks.

Arrange on 2 lined baking trays about 2 inches apart.

Allow to rise for 30 more minutes.

Coat with a quick egg wash before baking for 8-10 minutes until crispy and golden brown!

4. Spelt Pretzels

Another spin-off, this recipe uses spelt flour to make delicious soft pretzels!

Makes: 8 servings

Prep: 2 hrs. 10 mins

Cook: 10 mins

Ingredients:

- 1 package active dry yeast
- 1 cup warm water
- 1 tbsp. brown sugar
- 2 cups bread flour
- 1 ¼ cup spelt flour
- 2 tbsp. unsalted butter, cut into 1 inch pieces, at room temperature, plus more for greasing
- 2 tsp salt

Directions:

Preheat oven to 500 F.

Into a stand mixer, add in the warm water. Sprinkle on the yeast

Add in the brown sugar. Mix thoroughly and allow to bloom until foamy. This should take about 5 minutes.

Add in the flour, butter, salt, and continue stirring. On low speed, begin kneading the dough for a minute or until it forms a smooth ball. Continue kneading until the dough become pliant – about 5 minutes.

In a lightly greased bowl, place dough and cover with saran wrap. Set away to rise in a warm area for 90 minutes, until double.

Divide into 8 portions and roll out into desired shape – knots, buns, or sticks.

Arrange on 2 lined baking trays about 2 inches apart.

Allow to rise for 30 more minutes.

Coat with a quick egg wash before baking for 8-10 minutes until crispy and golden brown!

5. Olive and Garlic Pretzels

Let's get fancy with this delicious olive and garlic pretzel recipe!

Makes: 8 servings

Prep: 2 hrs. 10 mins

Cook: 10 mins

Ingredients:

- 1 package active dry yeast
- 1 cup warm water
- 1 tbsp. brown sugar
- 2 cups bread flour
- 1 ¼ cup spelt flour

- 2 tbsp. unsalted butter, cut into 1 inch pieces, at room temperature
- 2 tsp salt
- ½ cup pitted olives, roughly chopped
- 1 tbsp. garlic, minced
- 1 tbsp. fresh thyme, chopped
- ½ cup crumbled feta

Directions:

Preheat oven to 500 F.

Into a stand mixer, add in the warm water. Sprinkle on the yeast.

Add in the brown sugar. Mix thoroughly and allow to bloom until foamy. This should take about 5 minutes.

Add in the flour, butter, salt, and continue stirring. On low speed, begin kneading the dough for a minute or until it forms a smooth ball.

Add in the olives, garlic, and thyme and continue kneading until the dough become pliant – about 5 minutes.

In a lightly greased bowl, place dough and cover with saran wrap. Set away to rise in a warm area for 90 minutes, until double.

Divide into 8 portions and roll out into desired shape – knots, buns, or sticks.

Arrange on 2 lined baking trays about 2 inches apart.

Allow to rise for 30 more minutes.

Coat with a quick egg wash before baking for 8-10 minutes until crispy and golden brown!

Serve with crumbled feta.

6. Cinnamon-Raisin Pretzels

Looking for something sweet without going over the top? These cinnamon raisin pretzels are perfect with a cup of coffee!

Makes: 8 servings

Prep: 2 hrs. 10 mins

Cook: 10 mins

Ingredients:

- 1 package active dry yeast
- 1 cup + 2 tbsp. warm water
- 1 tbsp. brown sugar
- 2 cups bread flour

- 1 ¼ cup spelt flour
- 2 tbsp. unsalted butter, cut into 1 inch pieces, at room temperature, plus more for greasing
- ½ tsp salt
- ½ cup raisins
- 3 tbsp. cinnamon powder
- 2 tbsp. sugar + 1 tsp cinnamon.

Directions:

Preheat oven to 500 F.

Into a stand mixer, add in the warm water. Sprinkle on the yeast

Add in the brown sugar. Mix thoroughly and allow to bloom until foamy. This should take about 5 minutes.

Add in the flour, butter, salt, and continue stirring. On low speed, begin kneading the dough for a minute or until it forms a smooth ball.

Add in the raisins and cinnamon powder and continue kneading until the dough become pliant – about 5 minutes.

In a lightly greased bowl, place dough and cover with saran wrap. Set away to rise in a warm area for 90 minutes, until double.

Divide into 8 portions and roll out into desired shape – knots, buns, or sticks.

Arrange on 2 lined baking trays about 2 inches apart.

Allow to rise for 30 more minutes.

Coat with a quick egg wash and sprinkle with sugar and cinnamon mixture before baking for 8-10 minutes until crispy and golden brown!

7. Biscoff Pretzel Bites

Soft pretzels with biscoff cookie spread in the middle.

Makes: 12 servings

Prep: 2 ½ hrs.

Cook: 10 mins

Ingredients:

- 1 package active dry yeast
- 1 cup warm water

- 1 tbsp. brown sugar
- 3 ¼ cups bread flour
- ½ cup cold milk
- 2 tbsp. unsalted butter, cut into 1 inch pieces, at room temperature, plus more for greasing
- 2 tsp salt
- 1 ½ cups Biscoff spread

Directions:

Preheat oven to 500 F.

Into a stand mixer, add in the warm water. Sprinkle on the yeast

Add in the brown sugar. Mix thoroughly and allow to bloom until foamy. This should take about 5 minutes.

Add in the flour, butter, salt, and continue stirring. On low speed, begin kneading the dough for a minute or until it forms a smooth ball. Continue kneading until the dough become pliant – about 5 minutes.

In a lightly greased bowl, place dough and cover with saran wrap. Set away to rise in a warm area for 90 minutes, until double.

Place dough on a floured counter and divide into 12 equal portions.

Roll each piece into a rectangle. Place about 2 tbsp. of Biscoff in the center.

Pull the two edges of the dough together and pinch to cover. Ensure the Biscoff is completely covered and set onto a baking tray.

Repeat with the rest of the dough. Place dough pieces 2 inches apart.

Allow to rise for 30 more minutes.

Coat with a quick egg wash before baking for 8-10 minutes until crispy and golden brown.

8. Cheesy Jalapeno Pretzel Bites

Gooey melty cheese awaits you inside these pretzel bites!

Makes: 12 servings

Prep: 2 hrs. 40 mins

Cook: 10 mins

Ingredients:

- 1 package active dry yeast
- 1 cup warm water
- 1 tbsp. brown sugar
- 3 ¼ cups bread flour
- 2 tbsp. unsalted butter, cut into 1 inch pieces, at room temperature, plus more for greasing

- 2 tsp salt
- 2 cups grated cheddar
- 2 jalapeno peppers, sliced thinly
- Coarse salt for topping

Directions:

Preheat oven to 500 F.

Into a stand mixer, add in the warm water. Sprinkle on the yeast

Add in the brown sugar. Mix thoroughly and allow to bloom until foamy. This should take about 5 minutes.

Add in the flour, butter, salt, and continue stirring. On low speed, begin kneading the dough for a minute or until it forms a smooth ball. Continue kneading until the dough become pliant – about 5 minutes.

In a lightly greased bowl, place dough and cover with saran wrap. Set away to rise in a warm area for 90 minutes, until double.

Place dough on a floured counter and divide into 12 equal portions.

Roll each piece into a rectangle. Place a line of cheese in the center (about 2 tbsp.) and top with a 3-4 jalapeno slices.

Pull the two edges of the dough together and pinch to cover. Ensure the cheese is completely covered and set onto a baking tray.

Repeat with the rest of the cheese and dough. Place dough pieces 2 inches apart.

Allow to rise for 30 more minutes.

Coat with a quick egg wash before baking for 8-10 minutes until crispy and golden brown!

Top with coarse salt before serving!

9. Peanut Butter Pretzel Bites

Who doesn't love peanut butter? Add in soft pretzel bites and you have a winning recipe!

Makes: 12 servings

Prep: 2 ½ hrs.

Cook: 10 mins

Ingredients:

- 1 package active dry yeast
- 1 cup warm water
- 1 tbsp. brown sugar
- 3 ¼ cups bread flour
- 2 tbsp. unsalted butter, cut into 1 inch pieces, at room temperature, plus more for greasing

- 2 tsp salt
- 1 ½ cups creamy peanut butter

Directions:

Preheat oven to 500 F.

Into a stand mixer, add in the warm water. Sprinkle on the yeast

Add in the brown sugar. Mix thoroughly and allow to bloom until foamy. This should take about 5 minutes.

Add in the flour, butter, salt, and continue stirring. On low speed, begin kneading the dough for a minute or until it forms a smooth ball. Continue kneading until the dough become pliant – about 5 minutes.

In a lightly greased bowl, place dough and cover with saran wrap. Set away to rise in a warm area for 90 minutes, until double.

Place dough on a floured counter and divide into 12 equal portions.

Roll each piece into a rectangle. Place a line of peanut butter in the center (about 2 tbsp.)

Pull the two edges of the dough together and pinch to cover. Ensure the filling is completely covered and set onto a baking tray.

Repeat with the rest of the filling and dough. Place dough pieces 2 inches apart.

Allow to rise for 30 more minutes.

Coat with a quick egg wash before baking for 8-10 minutes until crispy and golden brown!

10. Nutella Pretzel Bites

Picky eaters are guaranteed to enjoy these delicious Nutella filled pretzel bites recipes!

Makes: 12 servings

Prep: 2 ½ hrs.

Cook: 10 mins

Ingredients:

- 1 package active dry yeast
- 1 cup warm water
- 1 tbsp. brown sugar
- 3 ¼ cups bread flour
- 2 tbsp. unsalted butter, cut into 1 inch pieces, at room temperature, plus more for greasing
- 2 tsp salt
- 1 ½ cups Nutella
- 4 tbsp. chopped hazelnuts

Directions:

Preheat oven to 500 F.

Into a stand mixer, add in the warm water. Sprinkle on the yeast

Add in the brown sugar. Mix thoroughly and allow to bloom until foamy. This should take about 5 minutes.

Add in the flour, butter, salt, and continue stirring. On low speed, begin kneading the dough for a minute or until it forms a smooth ball. Continue kneading until the dough become pliant – about 5 minutes.

In a lightly greased bowl, place dough and cover with saran wrap. Set away to rise in a warm area for 90 minutes, until double.

Place dough on a floured counter and divide into 12 equal portions.

Roll each piece into a rectangle. Place a line of Nutella in the center (about 2 tbsp.) and top with a tsp of crushed hazelnuts.

Pull the two edges of the dough together and pinch to cover. Ensure the Nutella is completely covered and set onto a baking tray.

Repeat with rest of the filling and dough. Place dough pieces 2 inches apart.

Allow to rise for 30 more minutes.

Coat with a quick egg wash before baking for 8-10 minutes until crispy and golden brown!

11. Coconut Cream Cheese Pretzel Bites

These pretzel bites are brilliants for an evening tea!

Makes: 12 servings

Prep: 2 ½ hrs.

Cook: 10 mins

Ingredients:

- 1 package active dry yeast
- 1 cup warm water
- 1 tbsp. brown sugar
- 3 ¼ cups bread flour
- ½ cup cold milk
- 2 tbsp. unsalted butter, cut into 1 inch pieces, at room temperature, plus more for greasing
- 2 tsp salt
- 1 ½ cups cream cheese frosting
- 4 tbsp. coconut flakes

- Sweetened coconut flakes for topping

Directions:

Preheat oven to 500 F.

Into a stand mixer, add in the warm water. Sprinkle on the yeast

Add in the brown sugar. Mix thoroughly and allow to bloom until foamy. This should take about 5 minutes.

Add in the flour, butter, salt, and milk, and continue stirring. On low speed, begin kneading the dough for a minute or until it forms a smooth ball. Continue kneading until the dough become pliant – about 5 minutes.

In a lightly greased bowl, place dough and cover with saran wrap. Set away to rise in a warm area for 90 minutes, until double.

Place dough on a floured counter and divide into 12 equal portions.

Roll each piece into a rectangle. Place a line of frosting in the center (about 2 tbsp.) and top with a tsp of coconut flakes.

Pull the two edges of the dough together and pinch to cover. Ensure the filling is completely covered and set onto a baking tray.

Repeat with rest of the filling and dough. Place dough pieces 2 inches apart.

Allow to rise for 30 more minutes.

Coat with a quick egg wash before baking for 8-10 minutes until crispy and golden brown!

Top with sweetened coconut flakes if desired before serving!

12. Cheesy Garlic Pull Apart Pretzels

Looking for game night recipes? Whip up these delicious pretzels pull apart!

Makes: 12 servings

Prep: 2 ½ hrs.

Cook: 10 mins

Ingredients:

- 1 package active dry yeast
- 1 cup warm water
- 1 tbsp. brown sugar
- 3 ¼ cups bread flour
- ½ cup cold milk
- 2 tbsp. unsalted butter, cut into 1 inch pieces, at room temperature, plus more for greasing
- 2 tsp salt
- 24 bocconcini mozzarella balls

- 1 tbsp. unsalted butter, melted
- 3 tbsp. chopped garlic
- 3 tbsp. chopped fresh flat-leaf parsley

Directions:

Preheat oven to 500 F.

Into a stand mixer, add in the warm water. Sprinkle on the yeast

Add in the brown sugar. Mix thoroughly and allow to bloom until foamy. This should take about 5 minutes.

Add in the flour, butter, salt, and continue stirring. On low speed, begin kneading the dough for a minute or until it forms a smooth ball. Continue kneading until the dough become pliant – about 5 minutes.

In a lightly greased bowl, place dough and cover with saran wrap. Set away to rise in a warm area for 90 minutes, until double.

Place dough on a floured counter and divide into 12 equal portions.

Roll each piece into a 4 inch circle.

Tear two of the mozzarella balls in half and pile them in the center of the dough.

Pinch together edges of dough to cover. Ensure the cheese is completely covered. Roll in your palms to ensure a proper sphere shape and set onto a lined baking tray.

Repeat with the rest of the cheese and dough. Place dough pieces 2 inches apart.

Allow to rise for 30 more minutes before baking for 5 minutes.

Remove from oven and coat with the melted butter and sprinkle with garlic.

Bake again for 5 minutes until crispy and golden brown.

Remove from oven and top with parsley before serving!

13. Pizza Pretzel Bites

This recipe combines classic pizza flavors inside a soft and fluffy pretzel!

Makes: 12 servings

Prep: 2 ½ hrs.

Cook: 10 mins

Ingredients:

- 1 package active dry yeast
- 1 cup warm water
- 1 tbsp. brown sugar
- 3 ¼ cups bread flour

- 2 tbsp. unsalted butter, cut into 1 inch pieces, at room temperature, plus more for greasing
- 2 tsp salt
- 1 cup pizza sauce
- 2 tbsp. olives, chopped
- ½ cup grated cheese

Directions:

Preheat oven to 500 F.

Into a stand mixer, add in the warm water. Sprinkle on the yeast

Add in the brown sugar. Mix thoroughly and allow to bloom until foamy. This should take about 5 minutes.

Add in the flour, butter, salt, and continue stirring. On low speed, begin kneading the dough for a minute or until it forms a smooth ball. Continue kneading until the dough become pliant – about 5 minutes.

In a lightly greased bowl, place dough and cover with saran wrap. Set away to rise in a warm area for 90 minutes, until double.

In the meantime, combine the pizza sauce and olives. Set aside.

Place dough on a floured counter and divide into 12 equal portions.

Roll out one portion into a rectangle. Place a heap of pizza sauce mixture in the center (about 2 tbsp.) and top with a tsp of grated cheese.

Pull the two edges of the dough together and pinch to cover. Ensure the filling is completely covered and set onto a baking tray.

Repeat with the rest of the dough. Place dough pieces 2 inches apart.

Allow to rise for 30 more minutes.

Coat with a quick egg wash before baking for 8-10 minutes until crispy and golden brown!

14. Pretzel Dogs

A classic appetizer, these pretzel dogs are loved by adults and children alike!

Makes: 12 servings

Prep: 2 ½ hrs.

Cook: 10 mins

Ingredients:

- 1 package active dry yeast
- 1 cup warm water
- 1 tbsp. brown sugar
- 3 ¼ cups bread flour
- 2 tbsp. unsalted butter, cut into 1 inch pieces, at room temperature, plus more for greasing

- 2 tsp salt
- 6 hotdogs, cut into 1 inch pieces.

Directions:

Preheat oven to 500 F.

Into a stand mixer, add in the warm water. Sprinkle on the yeast

Add in the brown sugar. Mix thoroughly and allow to bloom until foamy. This should take about 5 minutes.

Add in the flour, butter, salt, and continue stirring. On low speed, begin kneading the dough for a minute or until it forms a smooth ball. Continue kneading until the dough become pliant – about 5 minutes.

In a lightly greased bowl, place dough and cover with saran wrap. Set away to rise in a warm area for 90 minutes, until double.

Place dough on a floured counter and divide into 12 equal portions. Further divide each portion into 2 for a total of 24 pieces.

Roll out one portion into a rectangle. Place one piece of hotdog in the center and pull the two edges of the dough together. Pinch to cover. Ensure the hotdog is completely covered and set onto a baking tray.

Repeat with the rest of the cheese and dough. Place dough pieces 2 inches apart.

Allow to rise for 30 more minutes.

Coat with a quick egg wash before baking for 8-10 minutes until crispy and golden brown!

15. Parmesan Crusted Soft Pretzels

With this easy recipe, you can now make your favorite parmesan pretzels at home!

Makes: 12 servings

Prep: 2 ½ hrs.

Cook: 10 mins

Ingredients:

- 1 package active dry yeast
- 1 cup warm water
- 1 tbsp. brown sugar
- 3 ¼ cups bread flour
- ½ cup cold milk

- 2 tbsp. unsalted butter, cut into 1 inch pieces, at room temperature, plus more for greasing
- 2 tsp salt
- 1 cup grated parmesan cheese

Directions:

Preheat oven to 500 F.

Into a stand mixer, add in the warm water. Sprinkle on the yeast

Add in the brown sugar. Mix thoroughly and allow to bloom until foamy. This should take about 5 minutes.

Add in the flour, butter, salt, and milk, and continue stirring. On low speed, begin kneading the dough for a minute or until it forms a smooth ball. Continue kneading until the dough become pliant – about 5 minutes.

In a lightly greased bowl, place dough and cover with saran wrap. Set away to rise in a warm area for 90 minutes, until double.

Divide into 8 portions and roll out into desired shape – knots, buns, or sticks.

Arrange on 2 lined baking trays about 2 inches apart.

Allow to rise for 30 more minutes.

Coat with a quick egg wash and sprinkle with grated parmesan before baking for 8-10 minutes until crispy and golden brown!

Serve warm!

16. Cinnamon Sugar Pretzels

Cinnamon Sugar pretzels are a truly classic version of pretzels and loved by so many!

Makes: 8 servings

Prep: 2 hrs. 10 mins

Cook: 10 mins

Ingredients:

- 1 package active dry yeast
- 1 cup + 2 tbsp. warm water
- 1 tbsp. brown sugar
- 2 cups bread flour
- 1 ¼ cup spelt flour

- 2 tbsp. unsalted butter, cut into 1 inch pieces, at room temperature, plus more for greasing
- ½ tsp salt
- 3 tbsp. cinnamon powder
- 2 tbsp. sugar + 1 tsp cinnamon.

Directions:

Preheat oven to 500 F.

Into a stand mixer, add in the warm water. Sprinkle on the yeast

Add in the brown sugar. Mix thoroughly and allow to bloom until foamy. This should take about 5 minutes.

Add in the flour, butter, salt, and continue stirring. On low speed, begin kneading the dough for a minute or until it forms a smooth ball.

Add in cinnamon powder and continue kneading until the dough become pliant – about 5 minutes.

In a lightly greased bowl, place dough and cover with saran wrap. Set away to rise in a warm area for 90 minutes, until double.

Divide into 8 portions and roll out into desired shape – knots, buns, or sticks.

Arrange on 2 lined baking trays about 2 inches apart.

Allow to rise for 30 more minutes.

Coat with a quick egg wash and sprinkle with sugar and cinnamon mixture before baking for 8-10 minutes until crispy and golden brown!

17. Chocolate Pretzels

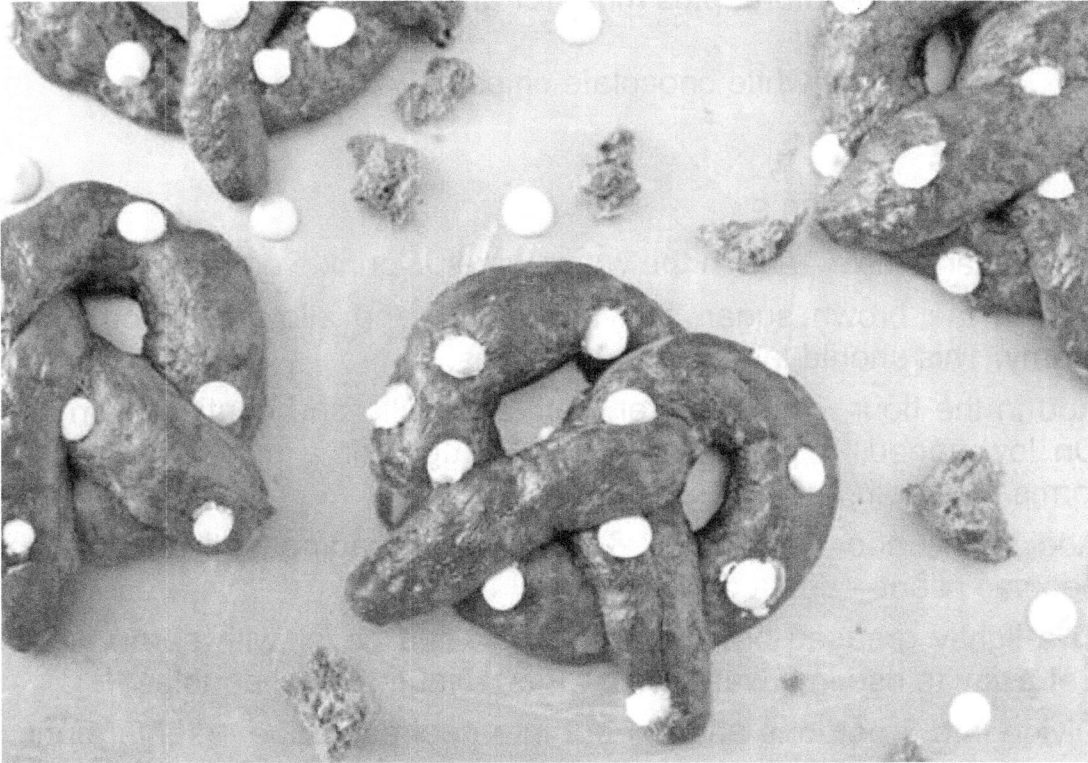

These chocolate pretzels are perfect for a children's get-together party!

Makes: 8 servings

Prep: 2 hrs. 10 mins

Cook: 10 mins

Ingredients:

- 1 package active dry yeast
- 1 cup warm water
- 1 tbsp. brown sugar
- 2 ½ cups bread flour
- ¾ cup cocoa

- ½ cup cold milk
- 2 tbsp. unsalted butter, cut into 1 inch pieces, at room temperature, plus more for greasing
- 2 tsp salt
- ¾ cups white chocolate chips

Directions:

Preheat oven to 500 F.

Into a stand mixer, add in the warm water. Sprinkle on the yeast

Add in the brown sugar. Mix thoroughly and allow to bloom until foamy. This should take about 5 minutes.

Add in the flour, cocoa, butter, salt, and milk, and continue stirring. On low speed, begin kneading the dough for a minute or until it forms a smooth ball.

Add in the chocolate chips & continue kneading until the dough become pliant – about 5 minutes.

In a lightly greased bowl, place dough and cover with saran wrap. Set away to rise in a warm area for 90 minutes, until double.

Divide into 8 portions and roll out into desired shape – knots, buns, or sticks.

Arrange on 2 lined baking trays about 2 inches apart.

Allow to rise for 30 more minutes.

Bake for 8-10 minutes until crispy!

Serve warm!

18. Choco Dipped Pretzels

Pretzels and gooey molten chocolate? Delicious!

Makes: 8 servings

Prep: 2 hrs. 10 mins

Cook: 10 mins

Ingredients:

- 1 package active dry yeast
- 1 cup warm water
- 1 tbsp. brown sugar
- 3 ¼ cups bread flour
- 2 tbsp. unsalted butter, cut into 1 inch pieces, at room temperature, plus more for greasing
- 2 tsp salt

- 1 cup dark chocolate chips
- 1 tbsp. butter

Directions:

Preheat oven to 500 F.

Into a stand mixer, add in the warm water. Sprinkle on the yeast

Add in the brown sugar. Mix thoroughly and allow to bloom until foamy. This should take about 5 minutes.

Add in the flour, butter, salt, and continue stirring. On low speed, begin kneading the dough for a minute or until it forms a smooth ball. Continue kneading until the dough become pliant – about 5 minutes.

In a lightly greased bowl, place dough and cover with saran wrap. Set away to rise in a warm area for 90 minutes, until double.

Divide into 8 portions and roll out into desired shape – knots, buns, or sticks.

Arrange on 2 lined baking trays about 2 inches apart.

Allow to rise for 30 more minutes.

Coat with a quick egg wash before baking for 8-10 minutes until crispy and golden brown!

In a saucepan, melt together the chocolate and butter until smooth.

To serve, begin dipping pretzels into the chocolate and lay on a wax paper lined tray.

Cool for 20 minutes before serving!

19. Almond Butter Pretzels

These delicious almond butter pretzels are the perfect breakfast dish or post-workout snack.

Makes: 8 servings

Prep: 2 hrs. 10 mins

Cook: 10 mins

Ingredients:

- 1 package active dry yeast
- 1 cup warm water
- 1 tbsp. brown sugar

- 2 cups bread flour
- 1 ¼ cup whole wheat flour
- 2 tbsp. unsalted butter, cut into 1 inch pieces, at room temperature, plus more for greasing
- 2 tsp salt
- 1 ½ cups creamy almond butter

Directions:

Preheat oven to 500 F.

Into a stand mixer, add in the warm water. Sprinkle on the yeast

Add in the brown sugar. Mix thoroughly and allow to bloom until foamy. This should take about 5 minutes.

Add in the flours, butter, salt, and continue stirring. On low speed, begin kneading the dough for a minute or until it forms a smooth ball. Continue kneading until the dough become pliant – about 5 minutes.

In a lightly greased bowl, place dough and cover with saran wrap. Set away to rise in a warm area for 90 minutes, until double.

Place dough on a floured counter and divide into 12 equal portions.

Roll each piece into a rectangle. Place a line of almond butter in the center (about 2 tbsp.)

Pull the two edges of the dough together and pinch to cover. Ensure the filling is completely covered and set onto a baking tray.

Repeat with the rest of the filling and dough. Place dough pieces 2 inches apart.

Allow to rise for 30 more minutes.

Coat with a quick egg wash before baking for 8-10 minutes until crispy and golden brown!

20. Philly Cheesesteak Pretzels

Everyone's favorite sandwich in a pretzel roll? Count us in!

Makes: 8 servings

Prep: 2 hrs. 10 mins

Cook: 10 mins

Ingredients:

- 1 package active dry yeast
- 1 cup warm water
- 1 tbsp. brown sugar
- 3 ¼ cups bread flour
- 2 tbsp. unsalted butter, cut into 1 inch pieces, at room temperature, plus more for greasing

- 2 tsp salt

Filling

- 2 tbsp. olive oil
- 1 green bell pepper, thinly sliced
- 1 onion, thinly sliced
- ½ tsp sea salt
- All-purpose flour for dusting
- 8 oz. thinly sliced roast beef
- 8 slices provolone cheese

Directions:

Preheat oven to 500 F.

To make the filling, heat a large pan with the oil. When hot, add in the pepper, onion, and salt. Cook until brown and tender for about 15 minutes.

Remove from pan and set aside.

Into a stand mixer, add in the warm water. Sprinkle on the yeast

Add in the brown sugar. Mix thoroughly and allow to bloom until foamy. This should take about 5 minutes.

Add in the flour, butter, salt, and continue stirring. On low speed, begin kneading the dough for a minute or until it forms a smooth ball. Continue kneading until the dough become pliant – about 5 minutes.

In a lightly greased bowl, place dough and cover with saran wrap. Set away to rise in a warm area for 90 minutes, until double.

Divide into 8 equal portions and being roll out one piece of dough into a large rectangle. Approximately 6.5 x 7.5 inches.

With the shorter end at the bottom, layer on one slice of the beef, 2 tbsp. of onion filling, and a slice of cheese along the lower half. Make sure to leave ½ an inch of dough border around the filling.

Fold the top of the dough over and press together the edges. Repeat with the rest of the dough pieces.

Arrange on 2 lined baking trays about 2 inches apart.

Allow to rise for 30 more minutes.

Coat with a quick egg wash before baking for 8-10 minutes until crispy and golden brown!

Serve warm!

21. Cheeseburger Pretzels

Another classic of a pretzel! These are great as a starter for a dinner party!

Makes: 8 servings

Prep: 2 hrs. 10 mins

Cook: 10 mins

Ingredients:

- 1 package active dry yeast
- 1 cup warm water
- 1 tbsp. brown sugar
- 3 ¼ cups bread flour
- 2 tbsp. unsalted butter, cut into 1 inch pieces, at room temperature, plus more for greasing

- 2 tsp salt

Filling

- 1 onion, thinly sliced
- ½ tsp sea salt
- 8 oz. cooked minced beef
- 8 slices American cheese
- Pickles, chopped
- Ketchup
- Mustard

Directions:

Preheat oven to 500 F.

To make the filling, heat a large pan with the oil. When hot, add in the pepper, onion, and salt. Cook until brown and tender for about 15 minutes.

Remove from pan and set aside.

Into a stand mixer, add in the warm water. Sprinkle on the yeast

Add in the brown sugar. Mix thoroughly and allow to bloom until foamy. This should take about 5 minutes.

Add in the flour, butter, salt, and continue stirring. On low speed, begin kneading the dough for a minute or until it forms a smooth ball. Continue kneading until the dough become pliant – about 5 minutes.

In a lightly greased bowl, place dough and cover with saran wrap. Set away to rise in a warm area for 90 minutes, until double.

Divide into 8 equal portions and being roll out one piece of dough into a large rectangle. Approximately 6.5 x 7.5 inches.

With the shorter end at the bottom, layer on 1 oz. of the cooked beef, 1 tbsp. of onion slices, and a slice of cheese along the lower half. Make sure to leave ½ an inch of dough border around the filling.

Top with desired toppings and fold the top of the dough over and press together the edges. Repeat with rest of the dough pieces.

Arrange on 2 lined baking trays about 2 inches apart.

Allow to rise for 30 more minutes.

Coat with a quick egg wash before baking for 8-10 minutes until crispy and golden brown!

Serve warm!

22. Crunchy Pretzel Rods

Make these in advance to have delicious pretzel snacks throughout the week.

Makes: 8 servings

Prep: 2 hrs. 10 mins

Cook: 10 mins

Ingredients:

- 1 package active dry yeast
- 1 cup warm water
- 1 tbsp. brown sugar
- 3 ¼ cups all-purpose flour

- 2 tbsp. unsalted butter, cut into 1 inch pieces, at room temperature, plus more for greasing
- 2 tsp salt

Directions:

Into a stand mixer, add in the warm water. Sprinkle on the yeast

Add in the brown sugar. Mix thoroughly and allow to bloom until foamy. This should take about 5 minutes.

Add in the flour, butter, and salt, and continue stirring. On low speed, begin kneading the dough for a minute or until it forms a smooth ball. Continue kneading until the dough become pliant – about 5 minutes.

In a lightly greased bowl, place dough and cover with saran wrap. Place dough in refrigerator and allow to cold rise for 8 hours or up to 24 hours.

Preheat oven to 325 F.

Divide into 48 equal portions and begin rolling out into a thin long shape.

Arrange on 2 lined baking trays about 2 inches apart.

Allow to rise for 30 more minutes.

Sprinkle with salt before baking for 20-30 minutes, testing for hardness.

23. Chocolate Dipped Hard Pretzels

A delicious hard pretzel variation – with chocolate! Yum!

Makes: 8 servings

Prep: 2 hrs. 10 mins

Cook: 10 mins

Ingredients:

- 1 package active dry yeast
- 1 cup warm water
- 1 tbsp. brown sugar
- 3 ¼ cups all-purpose flour
- 2 tbsp. unsalted butter, cut into 1 inch pieces, at room temperature, plus more for greasing
- 2 tsp salt

- 1 cup dark chocolate chips
- 1 tbsp. butter

Directions:

Into a stand mixer, add in the warm water. Sprinkle on the yeast

Add in the brown sugar. Mix thoroughly and allow to bloom until foamy. This should take about 5 minutes.

Add in the flour, butter, and salt, and continue stirring. On low speed, begin kneading the dough for a minute or until it forms a smooth ball. Continue kneading until the dough become pliant – about 5 minutes.

In a lightly greased bowl, place dough and cover with saran wrap. Place dough in refrigerator and allow to cold rise for 8 hours or up to 24 hours.

Preheat oven to 325 F.

Divide into 48 equal portions and begin rolling out into a thin long shape.

Arrange on 2 lined baking trays about 2 inches apart.

Allow to rise for 30 more minutes.

Sprinkle with salt before baking for 20-30 minutes, testing for hardness.

In a saucepan, melt together the chocolate and butter until smooth.

To serve, begin dipping pretzels into the chocolate and lay on a wax paper lined tray. You could now top with nuts or sprinkles if desired.

Cool for 20 minutes before serving!

24. White Chocolate Covered Pretzels with Sprinkles

Kids are going to absolutely love this! This recipe calls for white chocolate covered with sprinkles!

Makes: 8 servings

Prep: 2 hrs. 10 mins

Cook: 10 mins

Ingredients:

- 1 package active dry yeast
- 1 cup warm water
- 1 tbsp. brown sugar

- 3 ¼ cups bread flour
- 2 tbsp. unsalted butter, cut into 1 inch pieces, at room temperature, plus more for greasing
- 2 tsp salt
- 1 cup white chocolate chips
- 1 tbsp. butter
- ½ cup sprinkles

Directions:

Preheat oven to 500 F.

Into a stand mixer, add in the warm water. Sprinkle on the yeast

Add in the brown sugar. Mix thoroughly and allow to bloom until foamy. This should take about 5 minutes.

Add in the flour, butter, salt, and continue stirring. On low speed, begin kneading the dough for a minute or until it forms a smooth ball. Continue kneading until the dough become pliant – about 5 minutes.

In a lightly greased bowl, place dough and cover with saran wrap. Set away to rise in a warm area for 90 minutes, until double.

Divide into 8 portions and roll out into desired shape – knots, buns, or sticks.

Arrange on 2 lined baking trays about 2 inches apart.

Allow to rise for 30 more minutes.

Coat with a quick egg wash before baking for 8-10 minutes until crispy and golden brown!

In a saucepan, melt together the chocolate and butter until smooth.

To serve, begin dipping pretzels into the chocolate and lay on a wax paper lined tray. Toss on sprinkles while still wet.

Set for 20 minutes before serving!

25. Cheese Dipped Pretzels

These pretzels are absolutely delicious for a game night!

Makes: 8 servings

Prep: 2 hrs. 20 mins

Cook: 10 mins

Ingredients:

- 1 package active dry yeast
- 1 cup warm water
- 1 tbsp. brown sugar
- 3 ¼ cups bread flour
- 2 tbsp. unsalted butter, cut into 1 inch pieces, at room temperature, plus more for greasing

- 2 tsp salt
- 1 cup grated cheddar, melted

Directions:

Preheat oven to 500 F.

Into a stand mixer, add in the warm water. Sprinkle on the yeast

Add in the brown sugar. Mix thoroughly and allow to bloom until foamy. This should take about 5 minutes.

Add in the flour, butter, salt, and continue stirring. On low speed, begin kneading the dough for a minute or until it forms a smooth ball. Continue kneading until the dough become pliant – about 5 minutes.

In a lightly greased bowl, place dough and cover with saran wrap. Set away to rise in a warm area for 90 minutes, until double.

Divide into 8 portions and roll out into desired shape – knots, buns, or sticks.

Arrange on 2 lined baking trays about 2 inches apart.

Allow to rise for 30 more minutes.

Coat with a quick egg wash before baking for 8-10 minutes until crispy and golden brown!

To serve, begin dipping pretzels into the melted cheese and lay on a wax paper lined tray.

Set for 20 minutes before serving!

26. Tomato & Cheese Pretzels

Breakfast pretzels with tomato, cheese and basil.

Makes: 8 servings

Prep: 2 hrs. 10 mins

Cook: 10 mins

Ingredients:

- 1 package active dry yeast
- 1 cup warm water
- 1 tbsp. brown sugar
- 2 cups bread flour
- 1 ¼ cup spelt flour
- 2 tbsp. unsalted butter, cut into 1 inch pieces, at room temperature
- 2 tsp salt

- 1 large tomato, chopped
- ½ cup grated cheddar cheese
- 1 tbsp. fresh basil

Directions:

Preheat oven to 500 F.

Into a stand mixer, add in the warm water. Sprinkle on the yeast

Add in the brown sugar. Mix thoroughly and allow to bloom until foamy. This should take about 5 minutes.

Add in the flour, butter, salt, and continue stirring. On low speed, begin kneading the dough for a minute or until it forms a smooth ball.

Add in the tomato, cheese, and basil and continue kneading until the dough become pliant – about 5 minutes.

In a lightly greased bowl, place dough and cover with saran wrap. Set away to rise in a warm area for 90 minutes, until double.

Divide into 8 portions and roll out into desired shape – knots, buns, or sticks.

Arrange on 2 lined baking trays about 2 inches apart.

Allow to rise for 30 more minutes.

Coat with a quick egg wash before baking for 8-10 minutes until crispy and golden brown!

Serve warm!

27. Custard Pretzel Bites

Delicious homemade custard makes for a wonderful filling for these pretzel bites!

Makes: 8 servings

Prep: 2 hrs. 10 mins

Cook: 10 mins

Ingredients:

- 1 package active dry yeast
- 1 cup warm water
- 1 tbsp. brown sugar
- 3 ¼ cups bread flour
- ½ cup cold milk

- 2 tbsp. unsalted butter, cut into 1 inch pieces, at room temperature, plus more for greasing
- 2 tsp salt

Filling

- 2/3 cup cornstarch
- 2/3 cup custard powder
- 2/3 cup sugar
- 3 1/3 cup milk
- 1 tbsp. vanilla extract
- 1 1/2 cup thick cream
- 1/4 cup butter
- 3 egg yolks
- 2/3 cup pistachios (chopped)

Directions:

Preheat oven to 500 F.

Into a stand mixer, add in the warm water. Sprinkle on the yeast

Add in the brown sugar. Mix thoroughly and allow to bloom until foamy. This should take about 5 minutes.

Add in the flour, butter, salt, and continue stirring. On low speed, begin kneading the dough for a minute or until it forms a smooth ball. Continue kneading until the dough become pliant – about 5 minutes.

In a lightly greased bowl, place dough and cover with saran wrap. Set away to rise in a warm area for 90 minutes, until double.

To make the filling, combine the cornstarch, custard powder and sugar together in a saucepan and mix well. Add the milk, vanilla, and cream. Stir on low heat till the mixture has cooked and thickened. Add the butter. Cook for 5 minutes, continue stirring the mixture.

Remove from the heat and add the egg yolks. Mix well.

Add the pistachios and combine. Cover the custard and leave the custard to cool completely.

When dough has risen, Place dough on a floured counter then divide into 12 equal portions.

Roll each piece into a rectangle. Place about 2 tbsp. of custard in the center.

Pull the two edges of the dough together and pinch to cover. Ensure the custard is completely covered and set onto a baking tray.

Repeat with the rest of the dough. Place dough pieces 2 inches apart.

Allow to rise for 30 more minutes.

Coat with a quick egg wash before baking for 8-10 minutes until crispy and golden brown!

28. Jelly Pretzel Bites

Make your own jelly or use the store-brought if you're in a hurry! The recipe works well either way!

Makes: 24 servings

Prep: 2 hrs. 30 mins

Cook: 10 mins

Ingredients:

- 1 package active dry yeast
- 1 cup warm water
- 1 tbsp. brown sugar
- 3 ¼ cups bread flour
- ½ cup cold milk

- 2 tbsp. unsalted butter, cut into 1 inch pieces, at room temperature, plus more for greasing
- 2 tsp salt

Filling

- 1 cup strawberries chopped
- ½ cup sugar
- 1 gelatin sheet, bloomed

Directions:

Preheat oven to 500 F.

Into a stand mixer, add in the warm water. Sprinkle on the yeast

Add in the brown sugar. Mix thoroughly and allow to bloom until foamy. This should take about 5 minutes.

Add in the flour, butter, salt, and continue stirring. On low speed, begin kneading the dough for a minute or until it forms a smooth ball. Continue kneading until the dough become pliant – about 5 minutes.

In a lightly greased bowl, place dough and cover with saran wrap. Set away to rise in a warm area for 90 minutes, until double.

To make the filling, combine the ingredients together in a saucepan and cook until the strawberries have been crushed. Cool completely.

Once dough has risen, Place dough on a floured counter and divide into 12 equal portions. Divide each portion into 2 pieces for a total of 24 pieces.

Roll each piece into a rectangle. Place about 1 tbsp. of jelly in the center.

Pull the two edges of the dough together and pinch to cover. Ensure the jelly is completely covered and set onto a baking tray.

Repeat with the rest of the dough. Place dough pieces 2 inches apart.

Allow to rise for 30 more minutes.

Coat with a quick egg wash before baking for 8-10 minutes until crispy and golden brown!

29. Baklava Pretzel Bites

Delicious Middle Easter inspired filling takes these pretzel bites to another level!

Makes: 24 servings

Prep: 2 hrs. 10 mins

Cook: 10 mins

Ingredients:

- 1 package active dry yeast
- 1 cup warm water
- 1 tbsp. brown sugar
- 3 ¼ cups bread flour
- ½ cup cold milk

- 2 tbsp. unsalted butter, cut into 1 inch pieces, at room temperature, plus more for greasing
- 2 tsp salt
- ½ cup chopped walnuts
- ½ cup chopped pistachios
- ½ cup honey

Directions:

Preheat oven to 500 F.

Into a stand mixer, add in the warm water. Sprinkle on the yeast

Add in the brown sugar. Mix thoroughly and allow to bloom until foamy. This should take about 5 minutes.

Add in the flour, butter, salt, and continue stirring. On low speed, begin kneading the dough for a minute or until it forms a smooth ball. Continue kneading until the dough become pliant – about 5 minutes.

In a lightly greased bowl, place dough and cover with saran wrap. Set away to rise in a warm area for 90 minutes, until double.

To make the filling, combine the nuts and honey. Set aside.

Once dough has risen, Place dough on a floured counter and divide into 12 equal portions. Further divide each portion into 2 pieces for a total of 24 pieces.

Roll each piece into a rectangle. Place about a tbsp. of nut mixture in the center.

Pull the two edges of the dough together and pinch to cover. Ensure the filling is completely covered and set onto a baking tray.

Repeat with the rest of the dough. Place dough pieces 2 inches apart.

Allow to rise for 30 more minutes.

Coat with a quick egg wash before baking for 8-10 minutes until crispy and golden brown!

30. Mascarpone and Fig Pretzel Bites

Looking for a unique appetizer? Try out these delicious pretzel bites!

Makes: 8 servings

Prep: 2 hrs. 10 mins

Cook: 10 mins

Ingredients:

- 1 package active dry yeast
- 1 cup warm water
- 1 tbsp. brown sugar
- 3 ¼ cups bread flour
- ½ cup cold milk

- 2 tbsp. unsalted butter, cut into 1 inch pieces, at room temperature, plus more for greasing
- 2 tsp salt
- 1 ½ cup mascarpone cheese, whipped
- ½ cup fig slices

Directions:

Preheat oven to 500 F.

Into a stand mixer, add in the warm water. Sprinkle on the yeast

Add in the brown sugar. Mix thoroughly and allow to bloom until foamy. This should take about 5 minutes.

Add in the flour, butter, salt, and continue stirring. On low speed, begin kneading the dough for a minute or until it forms a smooth ball. Continue kneading until the dough become pliant – about 5 minutes.

In a lightly greased bowl, place dough and cover with saran wrap. Set away to rise in a warm area for 90 minutes, until double.

Roll each piece into a rectangle. Place about 2 tbsp. of mascarpone in the center and top with 1 fig slice.

Pull the two edges of the dough together and pinch to cover. Ensure the filling is completely covered and set onto a baking tray.

Repeat with the rest of the dough. Place dough pieces 2 inches apart.

Allow to rise for 30 more minutes.

Coat with a quick egg wash before baking for 8-10 minutes until crispy and golden brown!

Conclusion

Well, there you have it! Absolutely delicious pretzel recipes for you to try out at home. Make sure you try all of the recipes in this book and don't be afraid to try out your own variations! If you love these recipes, make sure to share them with your friends and family!

Made in the USA
Middletown, DE
16 June 2025

Dedication

I would like to thank my teachers and family for motivating me to write this book. My family taught me the good values of hard work, and my teachers have contributed to my education. Thank you to my brothers, Francis and Francisco. I would also like to reserve a special thanks to my mom and dad.

Preface

My name is Francesca Jen Tudla Tamano, and I am the author and illustrator of this book. I took high school Geometry. I started taking college classes when I was thirteen. By age fourteen / 1st year high school, I passed College Calculus with Analytical Geometry Honors.

I wrote this book based on extensive knowledge of geometry and my experience with math. This book will help any student succeed in high school geometry.

This book is organized into 11 lessons composed of sub-lessons.

Geometry Crash Course   By Francesca Tamano

Contents

Geometry Crash Course   By Francesca Tamano

Module 1: Introduction

Points, Lines, Planes

Euclidean Geometry is based on logical reasoning.

Coordinate geometry can be defined as the study of geometry using coordinates.

Geometry Terms:

Congruence: two figures are congruent when they are identical in size and shape

Undefined Terms: words that are not formally explained. Points and lines are considered undefined terms because they are usually understood without explanation.

Definition: an explanation

Defined term: can be explained using terms.

Equidistant: same distance from

Postulate or Axiom: statement that is true without proof.

Theorem: proved true using definitions, undefined terms, and postulates

Space: defined as a 3-D set of all points

Collinear: points that lie on the same line. Noncollinear points are not on the same line

Coplanar: points on the exact same plane

Undefined terms include:

Point: a location, which has no size or shape.

Line: made of points. There is one line through any 2 points

Plane: a flat surface that extends in all directions. There is exactly 1 plane through any 3 noncolinear points

Intersection: shared points that 2 or more figures have

Line Segments

Line segments have 2 endpoints.

You can write and solve equations to find the measurements of part of a line segment. State that AC = AB + BC.

$x + (2x + 3) = 4x - 12$

$$4x - 12$$

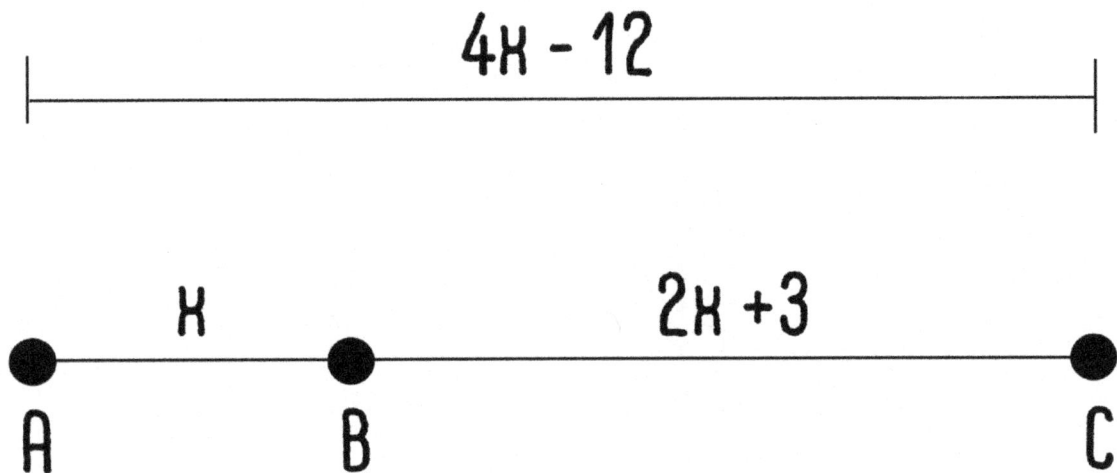

If two figures are the same size and shape, then they are congruent. Congruent means that the figures are identical in size and shape. 2 congruent segments will have the same measure.

If two-line segments have the same markings of congruence on them, then you can set their values equal.

Sketches: created without using tools (==no tools==)

Drawings: created using measuring tools (==yes tools==)

Constructions: created without measuring tools. Constructions use only compasses and straight edges (==some, but not all tools==)

Locating Points Using Ratios

The ratio is m: n to determine the coordinate of a point to divide a line

segment into a given ratio.

x_1 = starting endpoint

x_2 = ending endpoint

$$(\frac{nx_1 + mx_1}{m + n}, \frac{ny_1 + my_2}{m + n})$$

Example: The ratio is from AC to CB. Then, because the ratio starts with

AC, and then ends with CB, X_1 is the x-coordinate of A. x_2 is the x-

coordinate of B.

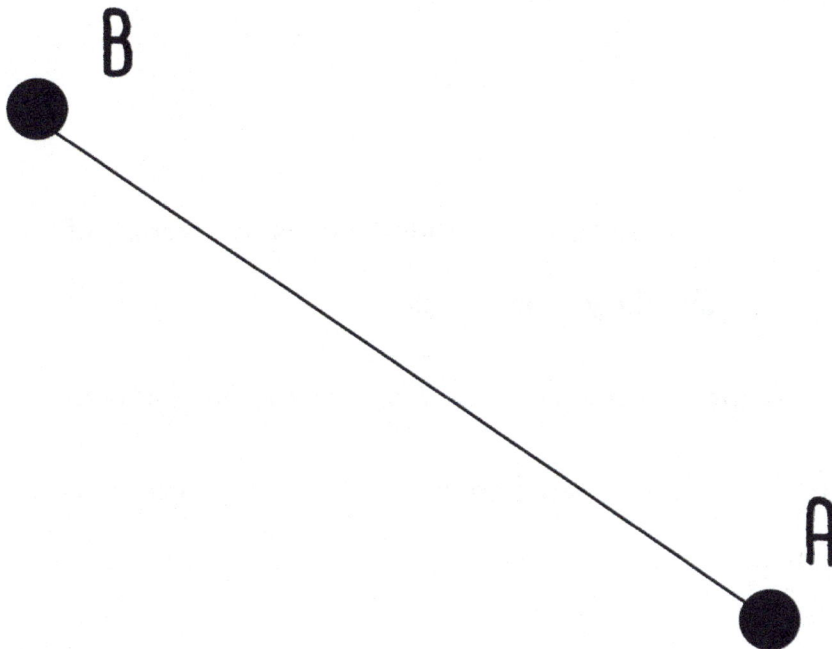

Midpoints and Bisectors

The point halfway between the endpoints is the midpoint. A point is equidistant from the other points if the point is an equal distance from the other points.

Midpoint Formula on a number line:

$$\left(\frac{x_1 + x_2}{2}\right)$$

Midpoint Formula on the coordinate plane:

$$\left(\frac{x_1 + x_2}{2}, \frac{y_1 + y_2}{2}\right)$$

The midpoint formulas can be thought of as the average of the x - coordinates and the y-coordinates.

Find missing coordinates given midpoint and one endpoint coordinate:

Find A if P = (3, 1/2) is the midpoint of AB and endpoint B has the coordinates (8, 3)

$$\left(3, \frac{1}{2}\right) = \left(\frac{x_1 + 8}{2}, \frac{y_2 + 3}{2}\right)$$

Set equal the x -value of the midpoint (3, 12) for the X value of the coordinate, and the y-value of the midpoint (3, 12) for the Y value of the coordinate.

A bisector is a segment that intersects something.

Locating Points Using Weighted Averages

A weighted average is the average of a set of values such as the values that hold different levels of importance.

The level of importance for each value is represented by a weight that is a constant greater than 0 (cannot be negative).

Weighted Average Formula on a Number Line:

x_1 = starting endpoint

x_2 = Last endpoint

w_1 = Weighted value for x_1

w_2 = Weighted value for x_2

You can add as many terms as you like.

Geometry Crash Course   By Francesca Tamano

$$\frac{w_1 x_1 + w_2 x_2}{w_1 + w_2}$$

Weighted Average Formula on the Coordinate Plane:

$$\left(\frac{w_1 x_1 + w_2 x_2}{w_1 + w_2}, \frac{w_1 y + w_2 y_2}{w_1 + w_2}\right)$$

You can add as many terms as you want to this formula.

The starting endpoint is (x_1, y_1)

The ending endpoint is (x_2, y_2)

Geometry Crash Course   By Francesca Tamano

Module 2: Angles and Geometric Figures

Angles and Congruence

<mark>Lines can cross to form angles.</mark>

Definitions:

Ray: A ray is the part of the line including a point on the line, or the ray's <mark>endpoint</mark>, and all the other points from that point on the line.

Rays can be named by calling the endpoint 1, then a point along the way 2

Opposite Rays:

<mark>2 collinear rays with a common point.</mark> Opposite rays form a <mark>180°</mark>.

Angle:

<mark>A pair of rays that have a common endpoint.</mark>

Angles, Sides, and Vertex:

<mark>The sides of the angle are the rays.</mark> The vertex is the common endpoint.

<mark>An angle divides a plane into 3 different parts.</mark>

Points can lie <mark>on the angles. In addition, points can be in the angle's interior or exterior.</mark>

Congruent Angles:

Geometry Crash Course   By Francesca Tamano

<mark>Angles that have the same measure</mark> are congruent angles.

You can use tools to copy an angle. To use a string, start by <mark>tying the end of the string to the pencil and thumbtacking down the other end.</mark>

Step 1: Given angle B, draw a ray on your paper.

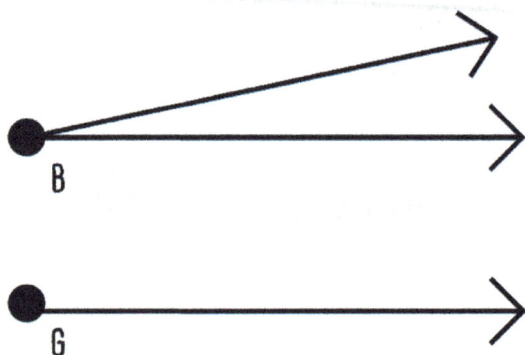

B

G

Step 2: Place thumbtack at vertex of angle B, and draw an arc that intersects the sides of angle B. Label points of intersection A and C.

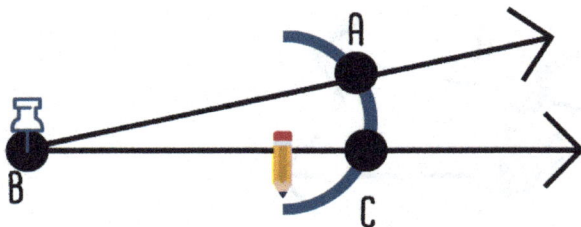

Step 3: Place the thumbtack at the endpoint of the ray and draw an arc that intersects the ray. Level the point of intersection H.

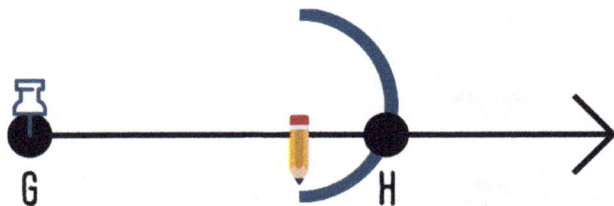

Step 4: Place thumbtack on C, and adjust string so that the pencil tip is on A

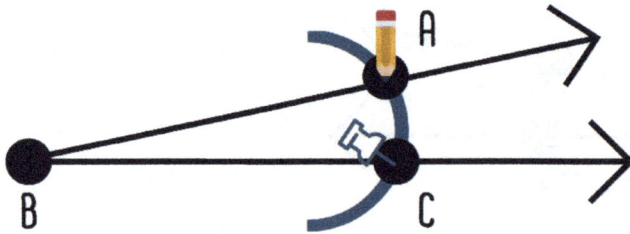

Step 5: Without altering the string length, put the thumbtack on the letter

H and construct an arc to cross the bigger arc.

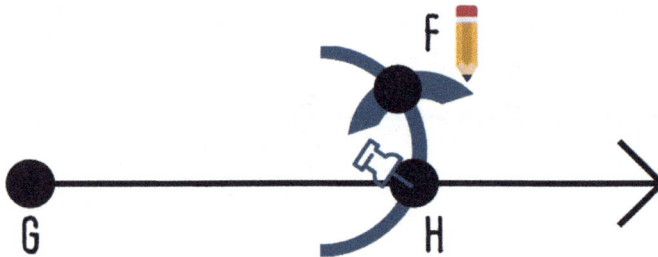

Step 6: Use a straightedge to draw ray GF.

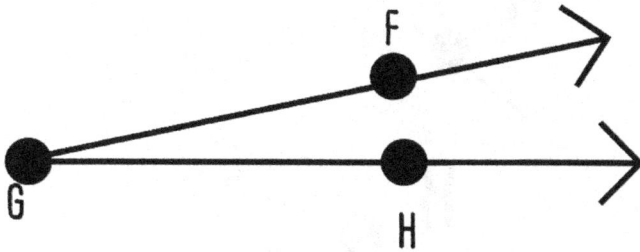

Now, you have 2 congruent angles.

A segment or ray that divides an angle evenly in 2 is an angle bisector.

How to Bisect an Angle:

1. Draw an angle on a sheet of tracing paper.

2. Fold the paper until the 2 rays you drew overlap. Then, unfold the

    paper.

3. Draw and label the crease in the middle.

Any angles that were bisected are congruent.

Special Angle Pairs:

There are 3 special angle pairs.

Two angles that lie on the same plane are adjacent angles with a common

vertex but no common interior angle points.

Geometry Crash Course   By Francesca Tamano

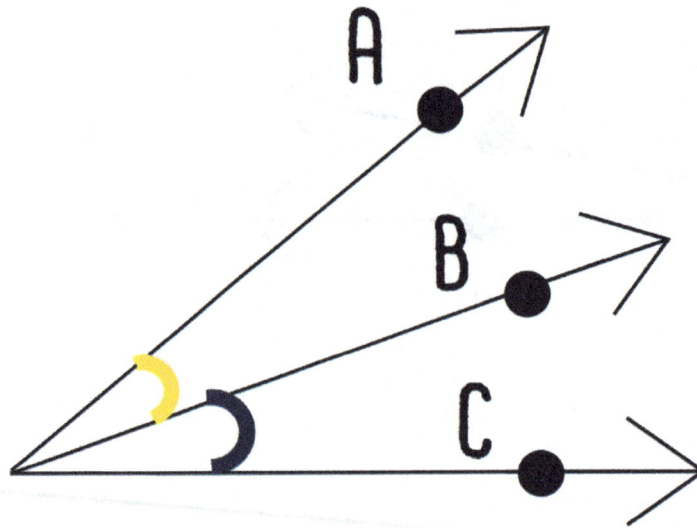

Linear Pair: <mark>pair of adjacent angles with noncommon sides that are opposite rays.</mark>

All linear pairs of angles are supplementary pairs.

Vertical Angles are the 2 nonadjacent angles formed by 2 <mark>intersecting</mark> lines (keyword: <mark>intersecting</mark>. There must be 2 lines that are <mark>crossing</mark> each other. The vertical angles will be the opposite angles formed). Vertical angles are always congruent.

Geometry Crash Course   By Francesca Tamano

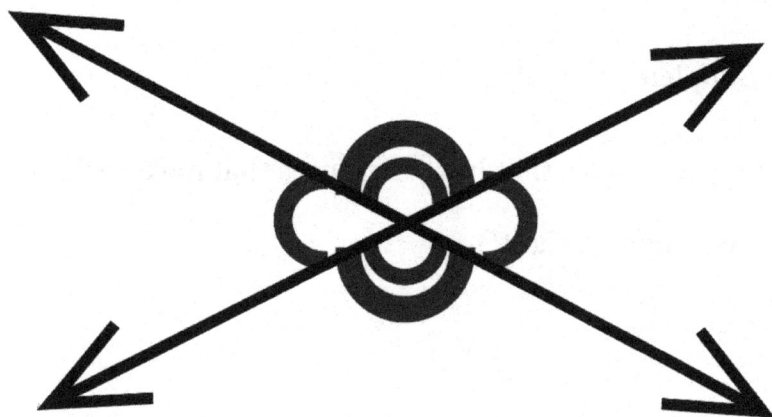

Angle Relationships

Complementary and Supplementary Angles

Complementary angles: two angles that ==have measures that have a sum of== ==90°== (Remember: A compliment is right!)

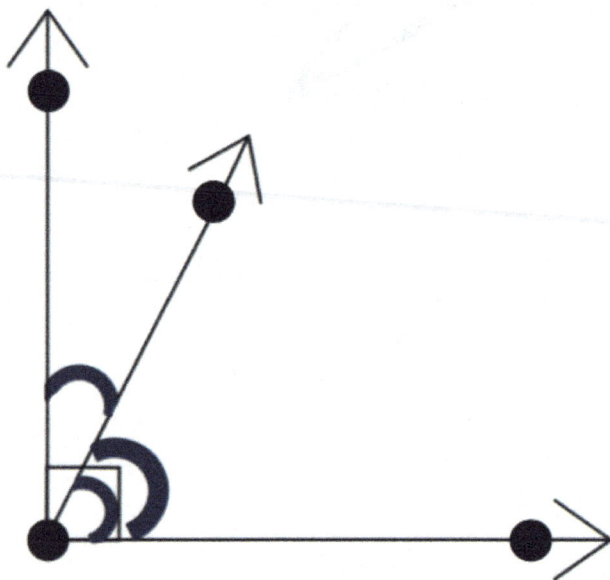

63°

27°

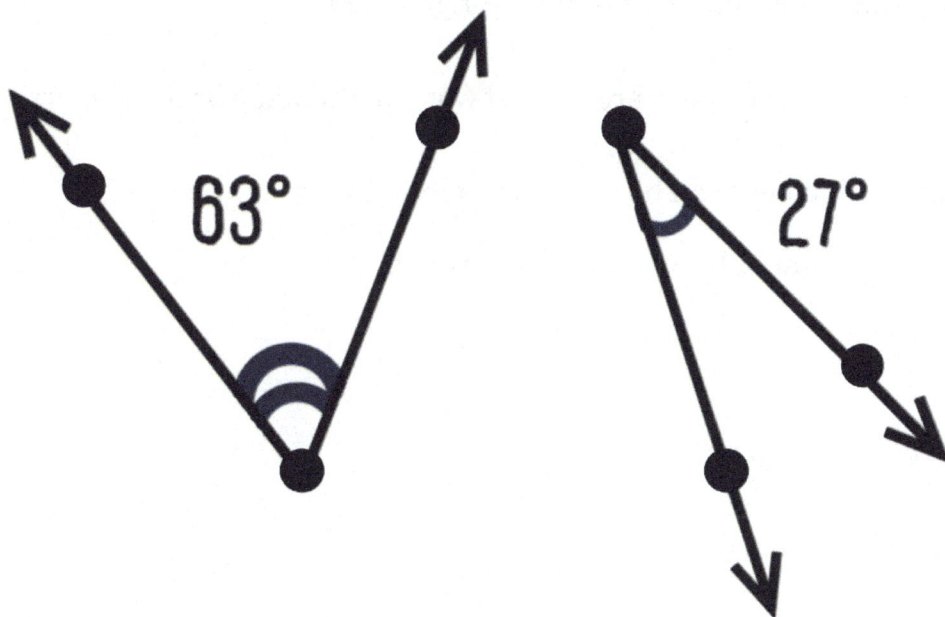

Supplementary angles: ==two angles that have measures the sum of 180°==

(they supplement each other!)

30°

150°

Lines, segments, or rays that intersect at ==right angles are perpendicular==.

The ==right-angle symbol (shaped like a small square)== indicates that lines are

perpendicular.

Geometry Crash Course   By Francesca Tamano

==Perpendicular lines intersect to form 4 right angles.==

==Congruent adjacent angles are formed when perpendicular lines intersect.==

Certain relationships can be assumed from a diagram, but most relationships cannot be assumed from a diagram.

Interpreting Diagrams:

What can be assumed:

- That all points shown are coplanar

- That points can be colinear

- That lines can intersect at a point

- The location of points (For example, if there is a line GJ, and point H looks like it is in the middle of the line, then we can say that point H is in between points G and J)

- Points that look like they are inside an angle are inside an angle

- That angles are adjacent angles

- Angles that are a linear pair

- That angles are supplementary (they add up to 180°)

What cannot be assumed:

- Lines that appear perpendicular may not be perpendicular

- Angles that appear congruent may not be congruent

- Segments that appear congruent may not be congruent

Geometry Crash Course   By Francesca Tamano

Two Dimensional Figures

Definitions:

A polygon is <mark>a closed plane figure</mark> with at <mark>least 3 straight sides.</mark>

Perimeter: <mark>the sum of the polygon's side lengths</mark>

Circumference: <mark>the distance around a circle</mark>

Area: the number of square units needed to cover a surface

Circumference, Perimeter, and Area Formulas:

Triangle:	Perimeter:
	$b + c + d$ Area: $\frac{1}{2}bh$
Square:	Perimeter: $4s$ Area: s^2

Geometry Crash Course   By Francesca Tamano

s	
Rectangle: Equiangular	Perimeter: $2l + 2w$ Area: lw
Circle:	Circumference: $2\pi r$ Area: πr^2

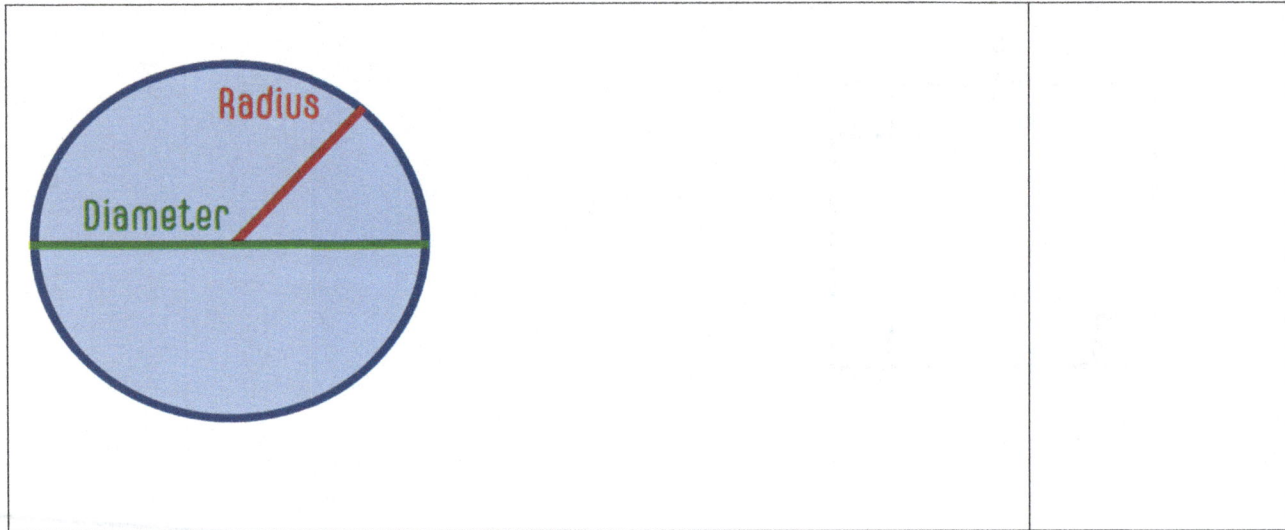

Reminder: A polygon is a figure on a plane with at least three angles and straight sides.

An equilateral polygon has all sides congruent. All equilaterals are equiangular. Equiangular means that the angles have the same measure.

This means that if a polygon has all sides congruent, then all the polygon's angles will also be congruent.

Geometry Crash Course   By Francesca Tamano

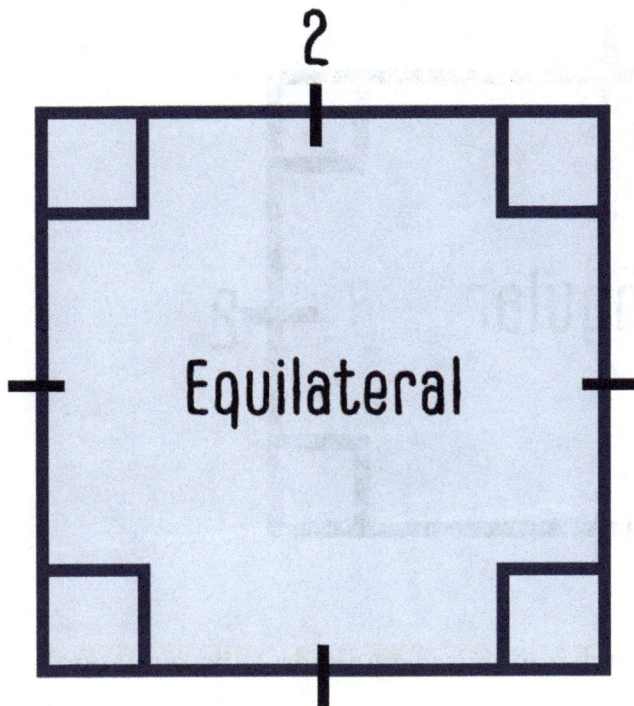

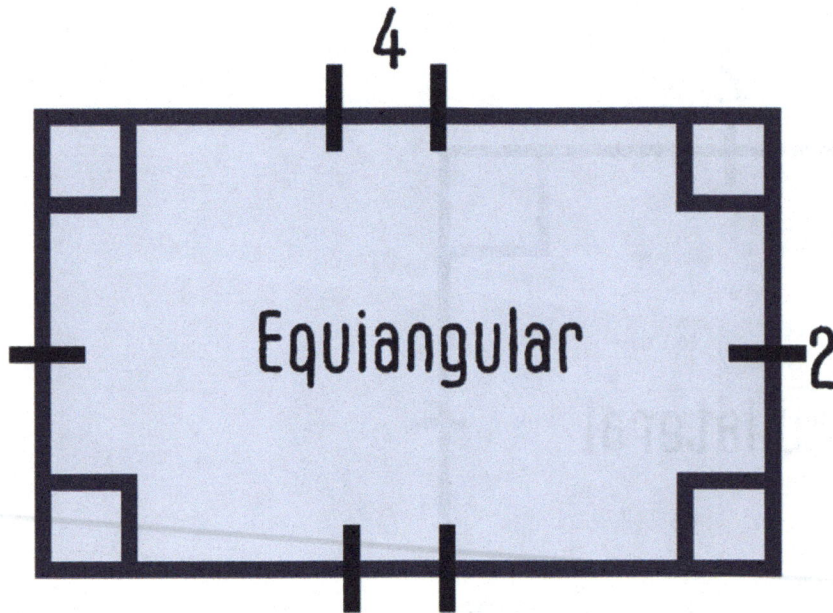

A regular polygon is a convex polygon that is equilateral and equiangular. It has all sides congruent to each other, and all angles congruent to each other (Example: square).

There are concave polygons and convex polygons. (Concave polygons, Cave In, on themselves)

Convex Polygon

Concave Polygon

Imagine if all the side lengths of the figure are extended. ==If any of those lines go into the polygon's interior, then the polygon is concave. Otherwise, if the extended side lengths do not intersect with interior points, then the figure is convex.==

Another way to tell convex and concave polygon apart is through angles.

All the interior angles of a concave polygon will be less than 180°.

If a polygon is concave, then at least one of its interior angles will be more than 180°.

Geometry Crash Course   By Francesca Tamano

The ==perimeter or area== of a polygon can be found using the ==Distance==

==Formula==. You can also use the Distance Formula to ==calculate the radius of==

==a circle==.

The Distance Formula:

$$\sqrt{(x_2 - x_1)^2 + (y_2 - y_1)^2}$$

First Point = (x_1, y_1)

First Point = (x_2, y_2)

To find the difference between the first point and the second point, insert

their values into the Distance Formula

Transformations in the Plane

Reflections:

<mark>In a reflection, all the preimage points and their corresponding points have the same distance from the reflection line. The segment that connects a point on the preimage to its corresponding point is perpendicular to the reflection line.</mark>

A reflection can be described as a function in which the preimage is reflected in the reflection line.

The points of the preimage are the input, and the points on the image are the output.

Here are the coordinate rules:

Reflections in the X–axis:	(x, y) to $(x, -y)$ x stays the same while y changes
Reflections in the Y-axis:	(x, y) to $(-x, y)$ y stays the same while x changes

Translations:

A translation is a function in which all the figure's points move the same distance in the same direction.

A preimage is translated along a translation vector. The translation vector describes the direction and magnitude of the slide if the magnitude is the vector length.

A vector in component form is like (7, 3), which means add 7 to the X value, and add 3 to the Y value.

Coordinate Rule:

To translate a point through the vector (a, b), add a to the x -coordinate and add B to the y-coordinate.

So,

(x, y) to $(x + a, y + b)$

Rotations: a rotation is a function that moves every point of a preimage through a specified angle and direction about a fixed point, called the center of rotation

Under a rotation, each point and its image are the same distance from the center of rotation.

The specified angle is called the angle of rotation. For example, the "angle of rotation" can be 270° clockwise, 10° clockwise, etc.

These are the Rotation Rules:

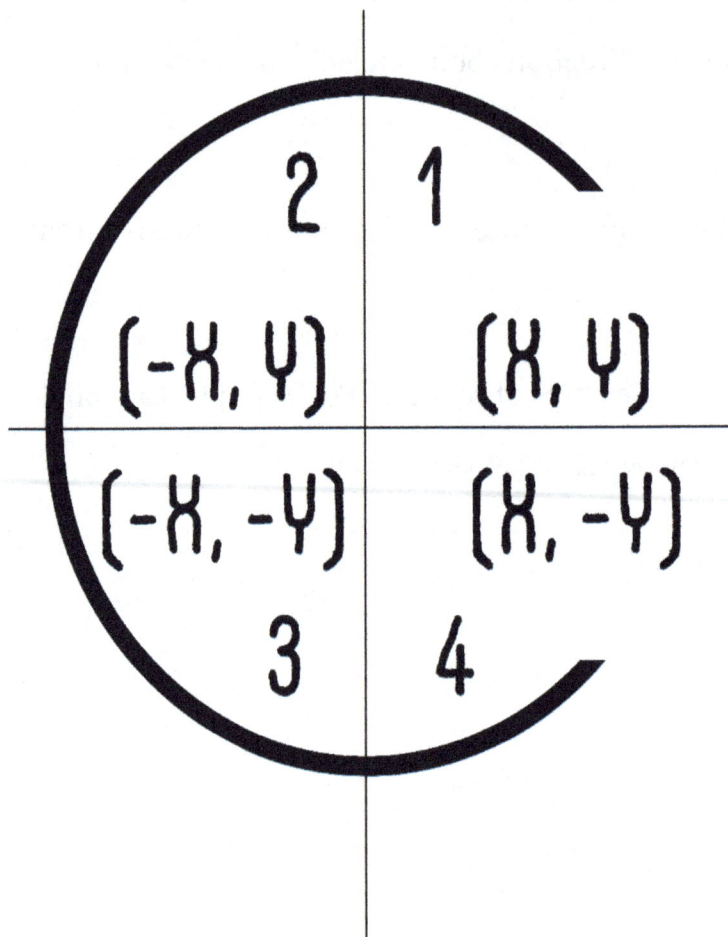

90^0 *counterclockwise* = (x, y) to (-y, x)

180^0 *counterclockwise* = (x, y) to (-x, -y)

270^0 *counterclockwise* = (x, y) to (y, -x)

Geometry Crash Course   By Francesca Tamano

Three-Dimensional Figures and Formulas

Definitions:

Polygonal: having more than 1 side

Polyhedron: a closed, 3-D shape made of polyhedron areas

Polyhedron face: flat surface

Polyhedron edge: the line segment where the faces intersect

Polyhedron vertex: the point along edge intersections

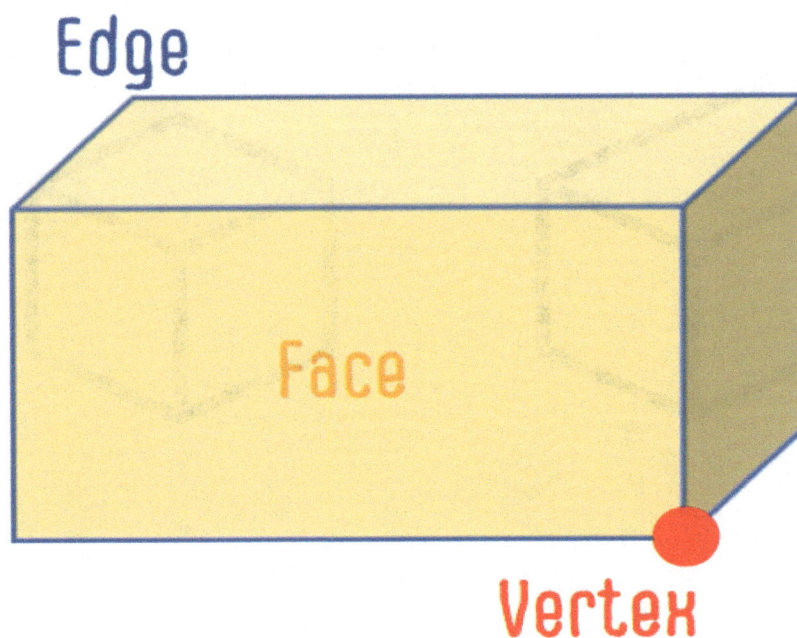

The bases of a prism or cylinder are the two parallel congruent faces of the solid.

The base of a cone or pyramid is the face of the solid opposite the vertex.

Types of Solids:

Prism: a polyhedron that has 2 parallel congruent bases, connected by parallelogram (a 4-sided polygon with 2 pairs of parallel sides) faces (each individual face itself is a parallelogram)

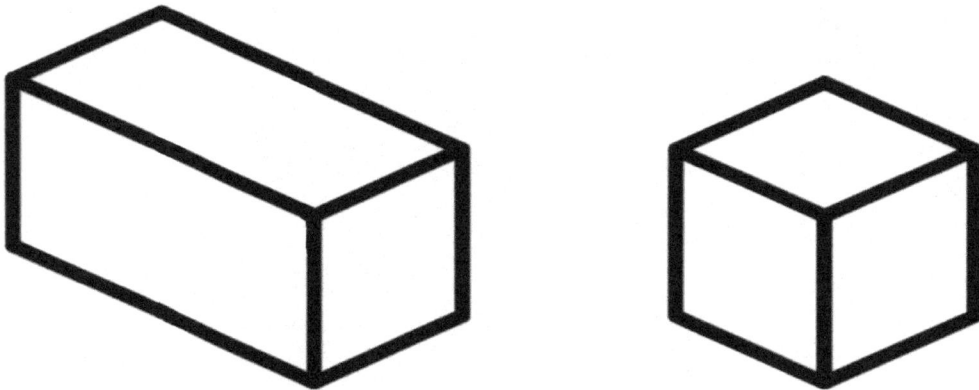

Pyramid: Has a base and at least 3 triangular faces that intersect at a vertex. A regular pyramid has a base that is a regular polygon.

Apex ●

Base

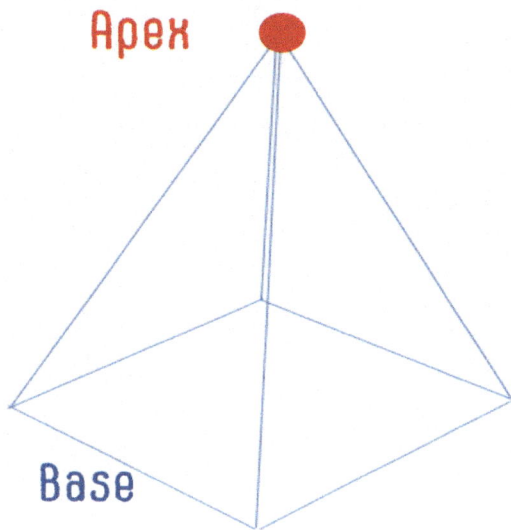

Cylinder: Has 2 parallel, congruent, and circular bases that are connected by a curved surface

Radius

Height

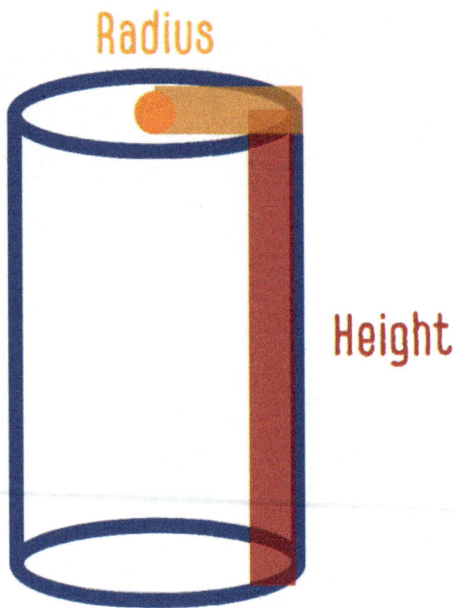

Cone: Has one circle base connected by the curved surface to the vertex

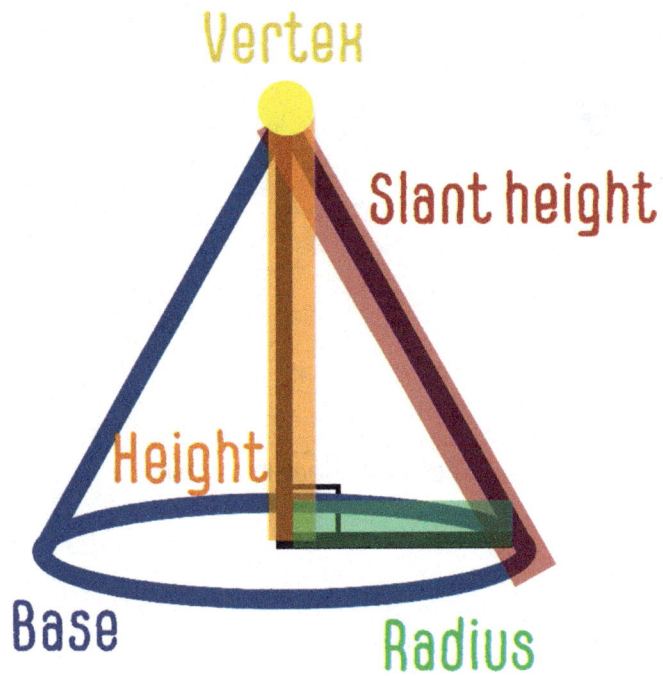

Sphere: a set of all points equidistant from the center of the sphere. A sphere has no edges, faces, or vertices.

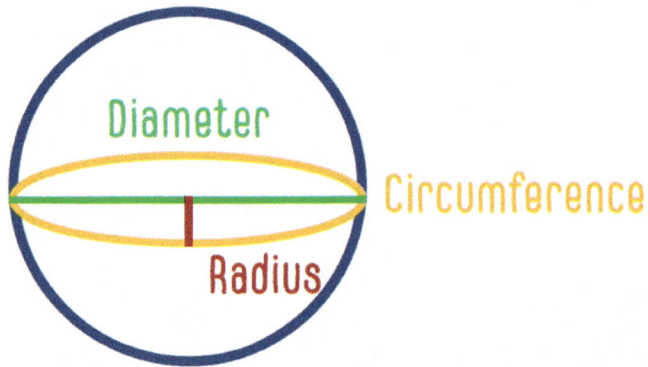

Right vs Oblique Prisms

In right prisms, then rectangular faces connect the bases.

In oblique prisms, or non-right, prisms, one face or more is not a rectangle

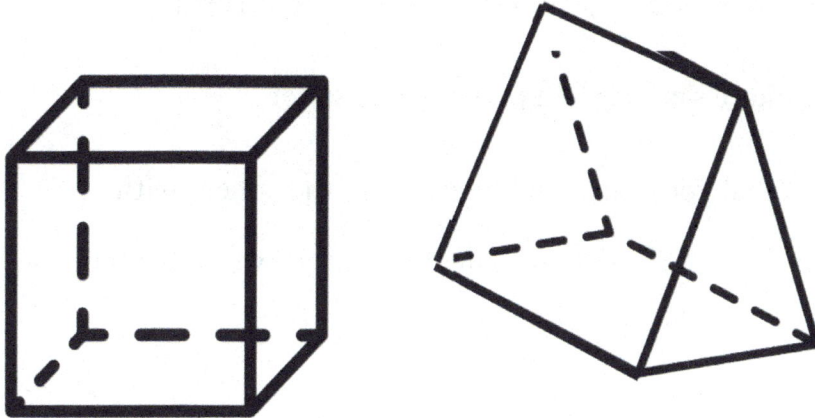

Polyhedrons, also known also polyhedral (plural), are named by their base shapes.

A regular polyhedron has faces that are all regular congruent polygons, and congruent edges.

More Definitions:

Geometry Crash Course   By Francesca Tamano

Surface Area: the sum of all the face areas

Volume: the measurement of the amount of space within a 3-d figure

Slant height of a pyramid or cone: the length of a segment with one endpoint on the figure's base edge and the other at the vertex point

Radius: from the sphere's center to a point on the sphere

Diameter: segment that goes through the center of the sphere with endpoints on either side of the sphere. The diameter is two times the radius.

Formulas:

h = height

P = perimeter of the base

b = area of the base

l = slant height

r = radius

Prism	Surface area: $Ph + 2b$
	Volume: bh

Right Regular Pyramid	Surface area: $\frac{1}{2}Pl + b$ Volume: $\frac{1}{3}bh$
Cylinder	Surface area: $2\pi h + 2\pi r^2 h$ Volume: $\pi r^2 h$
Right Cone	Surface area: $\pi rl + \pi r^2$ Volume: $\frac{1}{3}\pi r^2 h$
Sphere	Surface area: $4\pi r^2$ Volume: $\frac{4}{3}\pi r^3$

Geometry Crash Course   By Francesca Tamano

Module 3: Logic and Line Relationships

Conjectures and Counterexamples

An educated guess is a conjecture.

A counterexample disproves a statement. It shows that the statement is false by giving an example where the condition is satisfied, but the conclusion is not satisfied.

Example Statement: The square of an odd number is always even.

Counterexample: The square of 3 is 9.

Statements, Conditions, and Biconditionals

Definitions:

A statement is any sentence that is either true or false.

Truth value: whether a statement is true or false

Negation: if a statement is represented by p, then -p is the negation. -p has the opposite truth value.

Compound statement: 2 statements joined by the word and or

Conjunction: has the word AND. True when both statements are true. Written as

$$p \wedge q$$

Disjunction: true if at least 1 statement is true. Has the word OR

$$p \vee q$$

Conditional Statement: a compound statement that consists of a hypothesis and a conclusion, which is false when the conclusion is false but the hypothesis is true.

More Definitions: (related to conditions)

If then statement is a command statement of the form, if p, then q."

$$p \rightarrow q$$

Hypothesis: the phrase following the word if

Conclusion: the phrase following the word then

Converse: exchanging the hypothesis and conclusion of the conditional. If q, then p.

$$q \rightarrow p$$

Inverse: negating both the hypothesis and the conclusion

Contrapositive: negating both the hypothesis and the conclusion of the converse

More Definitions: Biconditionals

You can use biconditional statements to indicate exclusively in situations.

Biconditional statements are the conjunctions of a converse and its conditional.

Instead of writing this long statement,

$$(p \rightarrow q) \ \wedge \ (q \rightarrow p)$$

You can write this:

$$(p \Leftrightarrow q)$$

Read as p if and only q.

Important: To negate a statement with "for every" or "all," you can use "at least one" or "there exists." To negate the statement with "there exists," use the phrase "for every" or "for all."

Geometry Crash Course   By Francesca Tamano

Deductive and Inductive Reasoning

Deductive reasoning uses general rules, facts, definitions, or properties to reach specific valid conclusions from statements.

Inductive reasoning uses specific facts to reach general valid conclusions from statements.

An argument is valid if it is impossible for all the premises of it to be true, and for its conclusion to be false.

Law of Detachment: If p to q is a true statement, and p is true, then q is true.

Patterns = inductive

Facts = deductive

Law of Syllogism:

The Law of Syllogism can only be applied when one statement's conclusion is the same as another statement's hypothesis.

If

$$p \rightarrow q$$

and

Geometry Crash Course   By Francesca Tamano

$$q \rightarrow r$$

are true statements, then

$$p \rightarrow r$$

is a true statement.

True vs Invalid Conclusions:

A true conclusion reached using invalid reasoning is still invalid.

Geometry Crash Course   By Francesca Tamano

Writing Proofs

A postulate or axiom is a statement accepted as true without proof.

Below are postulates about Points, Lines, and Planes.

There is 1 line through 2 points
When there are 3 noncollinear points, then there is one plane
There are at least 2 points in 1 line
There are at least 3 noncollinear points in 1 plane
If 2 points (that are part of a line) lie in a plane, then the overall line with those 2 points lies in the plane
Two intersecting lines results in 1 point
Two planes intersecting results in 1 line

Two Column Proofs:

Definitions:

A proof is a logical argument in which all statements are supported by known facts and supporting reasons.

A two-column proof is a proof that contains the reasons and statements that are organized in a two-colon format.

You can also develop a deductive argument to prove a statement by building a logical chain of statements and reasons.

How to Write a Proof:

1. List given information. If needed, draw a diagram

2. Create deductive argument that links the information to the statement

3. Justify each statement with a reason

4. State what you have proven

Paragraph Proofs:

To prove a conjecture (educated guess), write a paragraph that explains why it is true.

Geometry Crash Course   By Francesca Tamano

Proving Segment Relationships

If A and C are collinear points, then point B is between point A and C if AB +BC = AC.

Segment Congruence:

Reflexive Property of Congruence: AB = AB

Symmetric Property of Congruence: EF = GH, then GH = EF

Transitive Property of Congruence. EF = GH, and GH = QS. Then, EF = QS.

Definitions:

Formal proof: a logical argument that includes all the steps needed to prove a relationship

Informal proof: a simplified proof that summarizes the logical reasoning needed to prove a relationship

Narrative proof: a type of informal proof that can include bullet points, calculations, or paragraphs.

Proving Angle Relationships

Every angle has a measure between 0° and 180°

D is in the interior of ∠ABC if and only if ∠ABD + ∠DBC = ∠ABC.

If the non-common sides of 2 adjacent angles form a right angle, then the adjacent angles have a sum of 90°

Reflexive Property of Congruence:	∠1 = ∠1
Symmetric Property of Congruence:	If ∠1 = ∠2, then ∠2 = ∠1
Transitive Property of Congruence:	If ∠1 = ∠2, and ∠2 = ∠3, then ∠1 = ∠3

Angles supplementary to the same angle are congruent

Angles complementary to the same angle are congruent

If two angles are vertical angles, then they are congruent

Perpendicular lines form adjacent and congruent angles

If a pair of angles are supplementary and congruent, then the pair of angles are right angles

Parallel Lines and Transversals

If a pair of lines does not intersect, then that pair of lines is either skew or parallel.

Definitions:

Parallel lines are coplanar lines that do not intersect.

Skew lines are lines that do not intersect

Parallel planes are planes that do not intersect.

A transversal is a line that intersect 2 or more lines in a plane at different points

Angle Pair Relationships

Consecutive Interior Angles	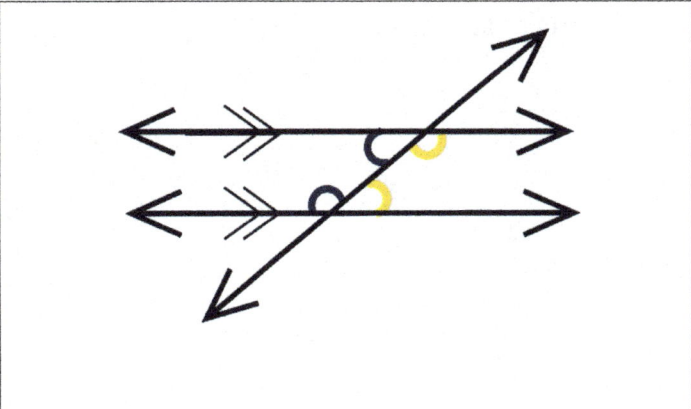
Alternate Interior Angles	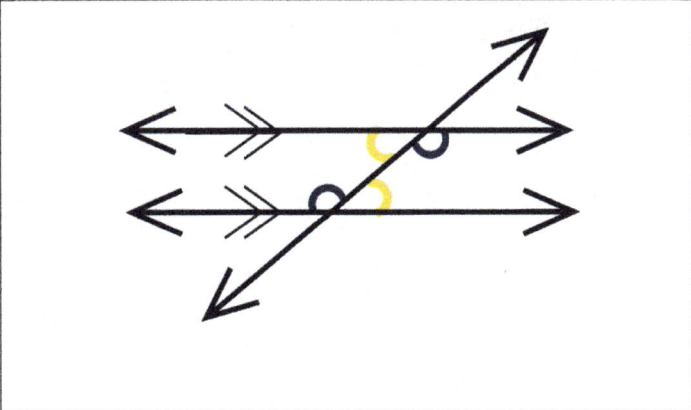
Alternate Exterior Angles	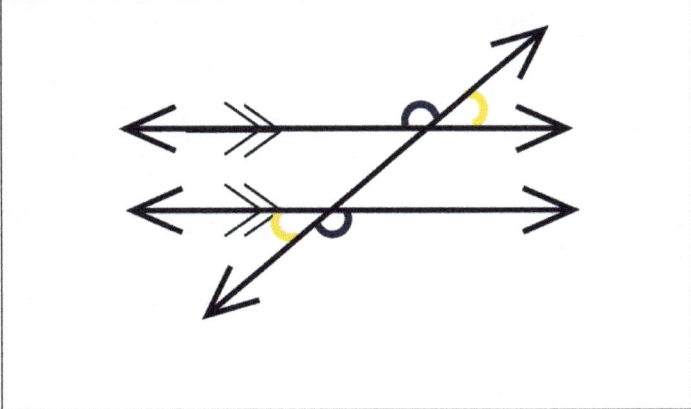

Vertical Angles	
Corresponding Angles	
Same Side Exterior Angles	

Complementary Angles	
Supplementary Angles	

If 2 lines are parallel and cut by a transversal, then there are special relationships in the angle pairs formed by the lines.

If a transversal cuts 2 parallel lines, then each pair of corresponding angles are congruent.

Geometry Crash Course   By Francesca Tamano

If a transversal cuts 2 parallel lines, ==then each pair of alternate interior angles are congruent.==

If a transversal cuts 2 parallel lines, ==then each pair of consecutive interior angles is supplementary.==

If 2 parallel lines are transversal, ==then each pair of alternate exterior angles is congruent.==

In a plane, if a line is perpendicular to one of the 2 parallel lines, then it is perpendicular to the other.

One way to prove proofs is called an indirect proof, which begins by assuming that the proof statement is false.

If a transversal intersects 2 lines so that the sum of the measures of the interior angles on same side of the transversal is less than 180 °, the lines will intersect on that side of the transversal.

Geometry Crash Course   By Francesca Tamano

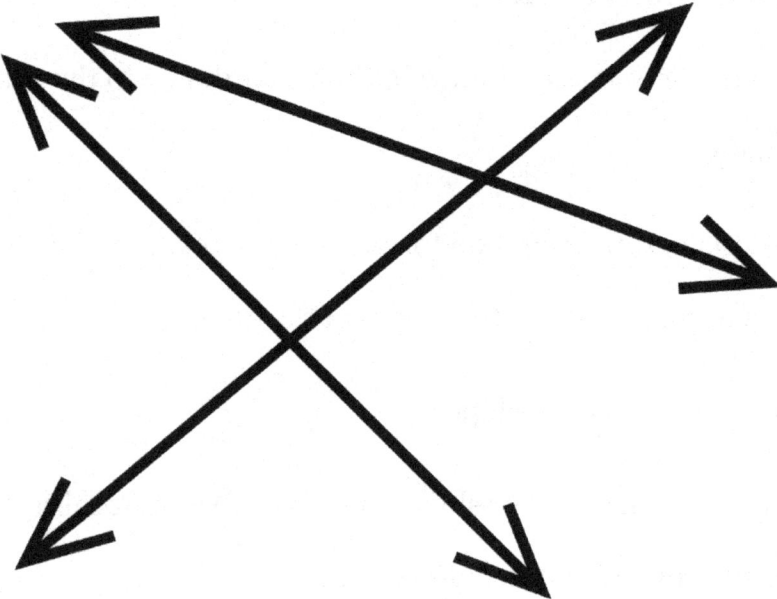

Geometry Crash Course   By Francesca Tamano

Slope and Equations of Lines

Slope is the ratio between the change in the y-coordinate to the change in the x coordinate.

The slope criteria outline a method for proving the relationship between lines based on a comparison of the slopes of the lines.

2 parallel lines have the same slope

2 lines are perpendicular if their slopes are negative reciprocals (e.g., Line AB has slope -2, while Line JI has slope 1/2).

Line Equations:

Slope-intercept form:	$y = mx + b$, where m is the slope and b is the y-intercept.
Point slope form:	$y - y_1 = m (x - x_1)$, where (x_1, y_1) is any point on the line.
Horizontal line:	$y = b$, where b is the y-intercept
Vertical line:	$x = a$, where a is the x-intercept

Proving Lines Parallel

Corresponding angles are congruent when the lines cut by the transversal are parallel. The converse of this relationship is also true.

A transversal that intersects parallel lines creates several pairs of congruent angles.

If a transversal intersects lines so that corresponding angles are congruent, then the lines are parallel.

If a transversal intersects lines in a plane so that alternate exterior angles is congruent, then the lines are parallel.

If a transversal intersects lines in a plane so that consecutive interior angles is supplementary, then the lines are parallel.

If a transversal intersects lines in a plane so that alternate interior angles are congruent, then the lines are parallel.

Geometry Crash Course   By Francesca Tamano

Perpendiculars and Distance

To determine the shortest distance between a line and a point, you must find the length of the segment that is perpendicular to the line through the point.

Parallel lines are equidistant, meaning that their distance between each other is always the same.

In a line, if 2 lines are equidistant from a 3rd line, then the 2 lines are parallel to each other. If they are both parallel to the 3rd line, then they are parallel to each other.

Geometry Crash Course   By Francesca Tamano

Module 4: Transformations and Symmetry

Reflections

Reflection in a vertical line: when a figure is reflected in a vertical line, the y coordinates stay the same

Reflection in a horizontal line: when a figure is reflected in a horizontal line, the x coordinates stay the same

Reflection in $y = x$

Interchange the x and y coordinates

Geometry Crash Course   By Francesca Tamano

Translations

A translation is a function in which <mark>all the points in a figure move in the same direction with the same distance as described by a translation vector.</mark>

Examples:

Point A (3,8) translated by (4, 7) is (7, 15).

Point Q (3, 1) translated by (8, 9) is (11, 10).

Point H (9, 3) translated by (6, 2) is (15, 5).

Rotations

Counterclockwise Rotation	Clockwise Rotation	Coordinate Rule
90° counterclockwise	270° clockwise	(x, y) to (-y, x)
180° counterclockwise	180° clockwise	(x, y) to (-x, -y)
270° counterclockwise	90° clockwise	(x, y) to (y, -x)

Geometry Crash Course   By Francesca Tamano

Compositions of Transformations

Composition of transformations: when a figure transforms and then undergoes another transformation

Glide reflection: the composition of a translation followed by a reflection in a line parallel to the translation vector

An isometry is a reflection, translation, or rotation.

An isometry is the composition of multiple isometries.

The compositions of 2 reflections can result in the same image as a translation or rotation.

A translation vector that is perpendicular and twice the distance between the 2 lines may be used to describe the composition of 2 reflections.

Image below not to scale·

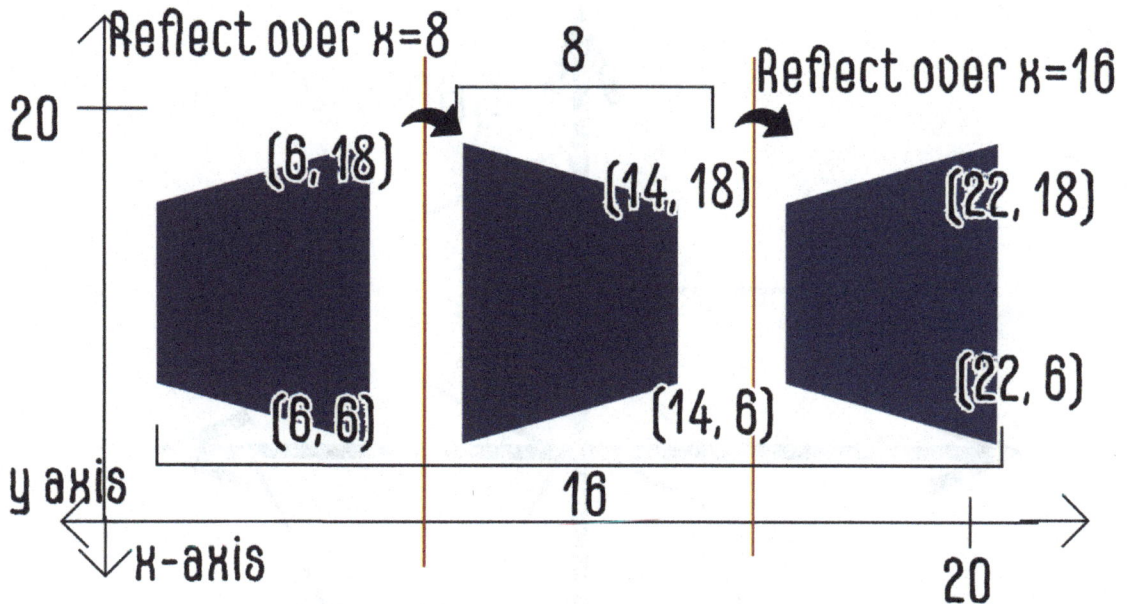

The composition of 2 reflections in intersecting lines can be described by a rotation that is about the point where the lines intersect and through an angle that is twice the measure of the acute or right angle formed by the lines.

The rotation centers at point X. It is at an angle of 120°.

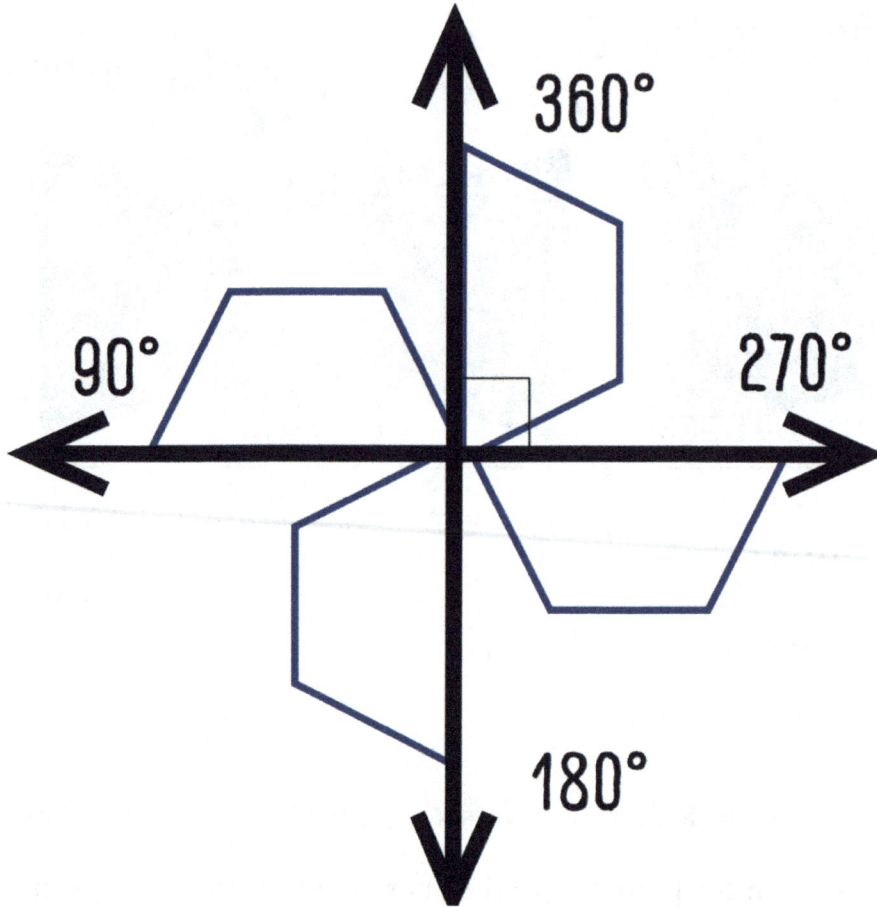

Geometry Crash Course   By Francesca Tamano

Symmetry

Types of Tessellations

A tessellation is a repeating pattern of one or more figures that covers a plane with no overlapping or empty spaces. The sum of the measures of the angles around a vertex of a tessellation is 360.

One type of regular polygon forms a regular tessellation. A regular polygon will tessellate if it has an interior angle measure that is a factor of 360 (180°, 120°, etc.)

Geometry Crash Course   By Francesca Tamano

<mark>Not all polygons have to be regular to tessellate the plane.</mark> <mark>Any triangle can tessellate a plane</mark> because its interior angles add up to 180°. <mark>Any quadrilateral can tesselate a plane</mark>

A figure that has symmetry can be transformed onto itself.

Line Symmetry:

A figure has line <mark>symmetry if each side of the figure matches the other side exactly.</mark>

Rotational Symmetry: if a figure can look the same after a rotation less than 360°

The point around which a figure can be rotated onto itself is called the center of symmetry.

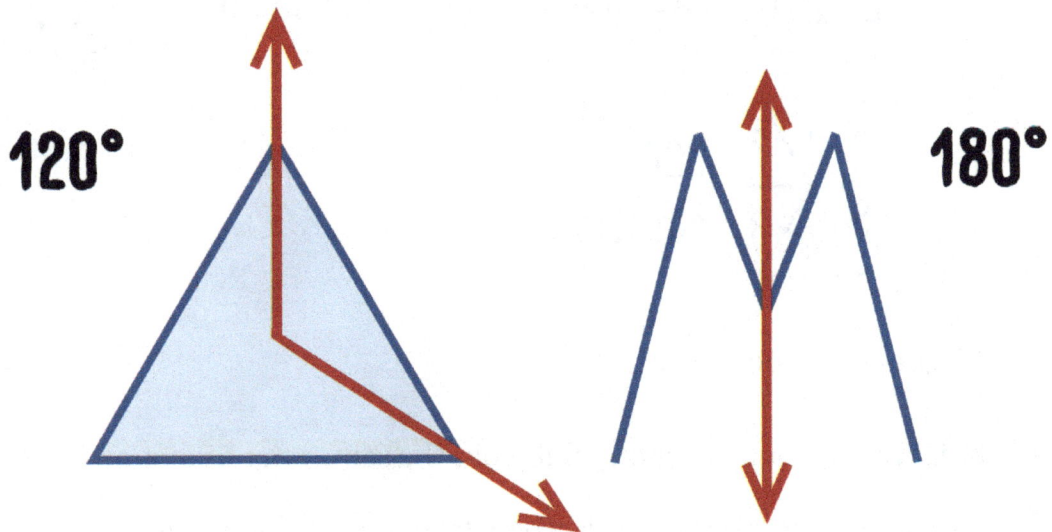

120° **180°**

The number of times that a figure looks the same as it rotates is the order of symmetry. The magnitude of symmetry is the smallest angle through which the figure can be rotated to be mapped onto itself

(The order of the diagram below is 6, and the magnitude is 60°)

Geometry Crash Course   By Francesca Tamano

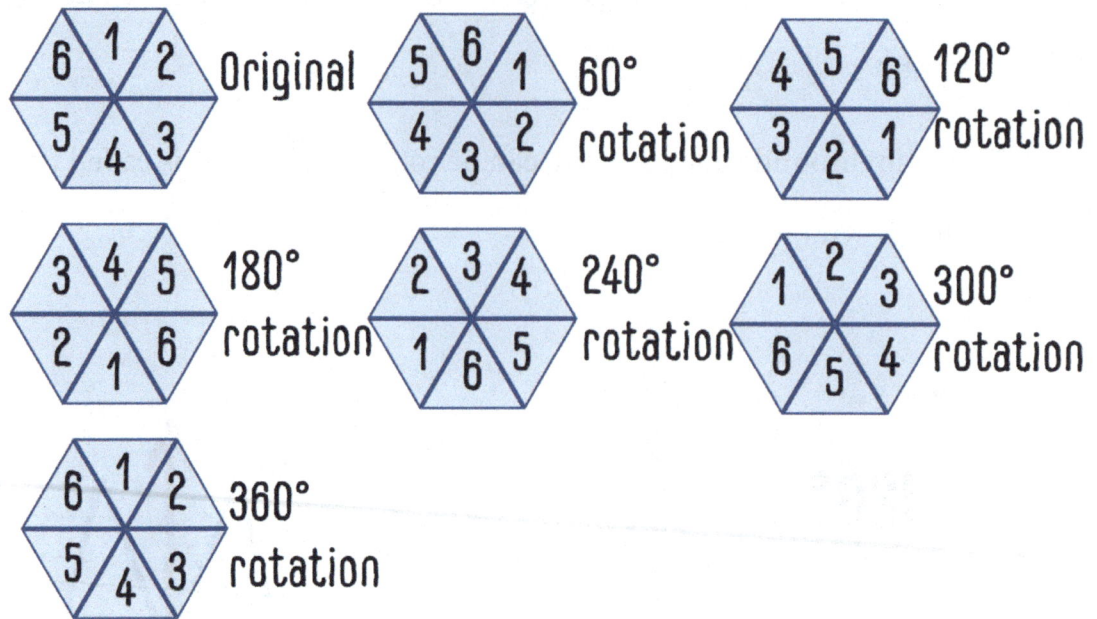

Magnitude = 360/order

A figure has point symmetry if it looks the same after a rotation of 180°.

Simplified, point symmetry is when given a central point, every point on the opposite side is the same distance from the central point. The center of symmetry in the figure is called the point of symmetry.

Translational symmetry:

A pattern with translational symmetry can be created by translating a group of figures without reflection or rotation.

Module 5: Triangles and Congruence

Angles of Triangles

An interior angle is the angle at the vertex of a triangle. All triangles have 3 interior angles that add up to 180°.

A scalene triangle:

All sides and angles have different measures

Isosceles triangle:

2 congruent angles and 2 congruent sides

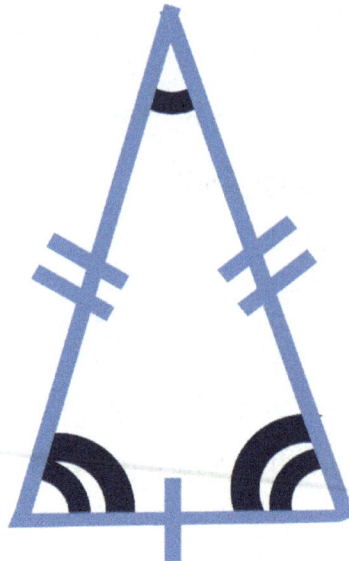

Equilateral triangle:

<mark>3 congruent sides and angles</mark>

Geometry Crash Course   By Francesca Tamano

Acute angles: have a measure of <mark>less than 90°</mark>

Right angles: have a measure <mark>equaling 90°</mark>

Obtuse angles: have a measure <mark>from 90° to 180°</mark>

Exterior angles: an exterior angle of a triangle is an angle formed by the side of the triangle and the extension of an adjacent side. A triangle has 3 exterior angles. <mark>The sum of the 3 Exterior Triangle Angles is 360°.</mark>

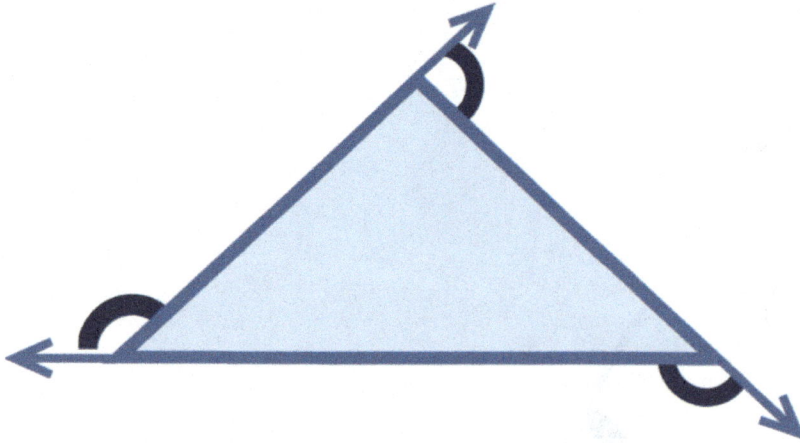

Hence, it must be the original length of one side, and the extension of a different side.

Remote interior angles: ==each exterior angle of a triangle has 2 remote interior angles that are not adjacent to the exterior angle.==

==The measure of a triangle's exterior measure equals the sums of the measures of the 2 remote interior angles==

A corollary is a theorem with a proof that flows as a direct result of another theorem (it uses another theorem in its reasoning)

Right triangles have complementary acute angles

There can be at most one right or obtuse angle in a triangle

Geometry Crash Course   By Francesca Tamano

Geometry Crash Course   By Francesca Tamano

Congruent Triangles

The principle of superposition states that 2 figures are congruent if there are rigid transformations that map 1 figure onto the other

In 2 congruent polygons, all the parts of a polygon are congruent to the corresponding parts.

If 2 angles of one triangle are congruent to 2 angles of a second triangle. Then the third angles of the triangle are congruent.

Properties of triangle congruence:

Reflexive property of triangle congruence: a triangle is congruent to itself

$$\triangle ABC = \triangle ABC$$

Symmetric property of triangle congruence: (if one side of the equation is equal to the other side, then the 2 sides are interchangeable)

If $\triangle ABC = \triangle EFG$, then $\triangle EFG = \triangle ABC$

Transitive Property of triangle congruence: (Basically, if a=b, and b=c, then a=c/ If a box has 3 letters, it has the same amount as a mailbox with 3 letters, which has the same amount as a package with 3 letters, so the box

has the same number of letters as the package)

If $\Delta ABC = \Delta EFG$, and $\Delta EFG = \Delta JKL$, then $\Delta ABC = \Delta JKL$.

Definition: the interior angle formed by ==2 adjacent sides of a triangle is==

==called the included angle.==

Proving Triangles Congruent: SSS, SAS

Side Side Side Congruence

==If 3 sides of a triangle are congruent to 3 sides of another triangle, then the==

==triangles are congruent.==

Side Angle Side Congruence

Geometry Crash Course   By Francesca Tamano

If 2 sides and the included angle of a triangle are congruent to the 2 sides

and included angle of another triangle, then the triangles are congruent.

Proving Triangles Congruent: ASA, AAS

An included side is the side of a triangle between 2 angles.

Angle Side Angle Congruence

If 2 angles and the included side of one triangle are congruent to 2 angles and the included side of another triangles, then the 2 triangles are congruent

Angle Angle Side Congruence

If 2 angles and the nonincluded side of a triangle are congruent to the corresponding 2 angles and nonincluded side of another triangle, then the 2 triangles are congruent to each other.

Geometry Crash Course   By Francesca Tamano

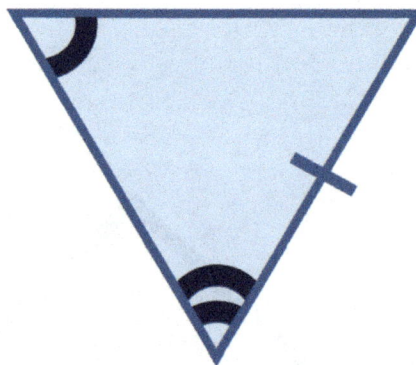

Proving Right Triangles Congruent

Because right triangles are congruent, ==we can use the SAS AAS, and ASA criteria for congruence to prove 4 theorems related to congruence in right triangles.==

==Remember, these theorems only apply to right triangles!==

Leg Leg Congruence

==If the legs of one right triangle are congruent to the corresponding legs of another right triangle, then the triangles are congruent.==

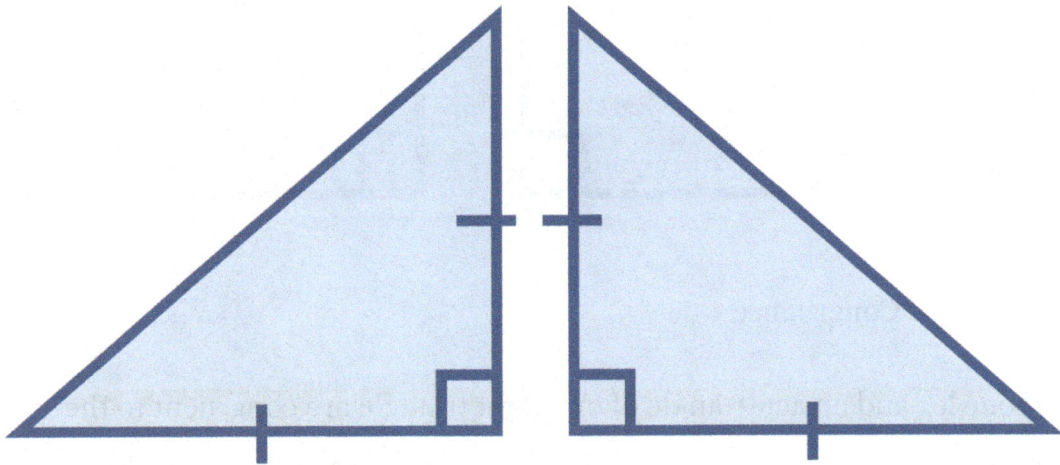

Hypotenuse Angle Congruence

Geometry Crash Course   By Francesca Tamano

==If the hypotenuse and acute angle of one right triangle are congruent to the corresponding hypotenuse and acute angle of another right triangle, then the triangles are congruent.==

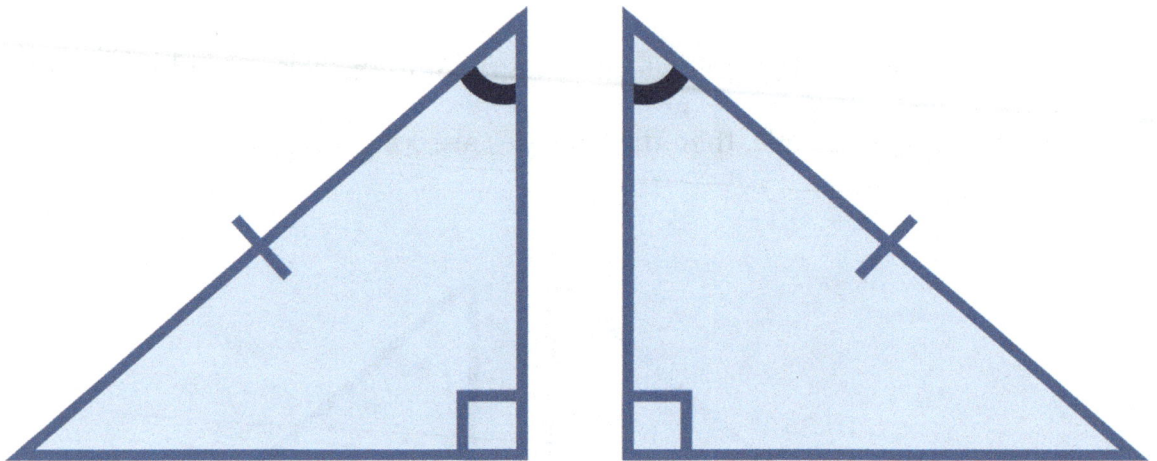

Leg Angle Congruence

==If one leg and an acute angle of one right triangle are congruent to the corresponding leg and acute angle of another right triangle, then the triangles are congruent. (E is the acute angle)==

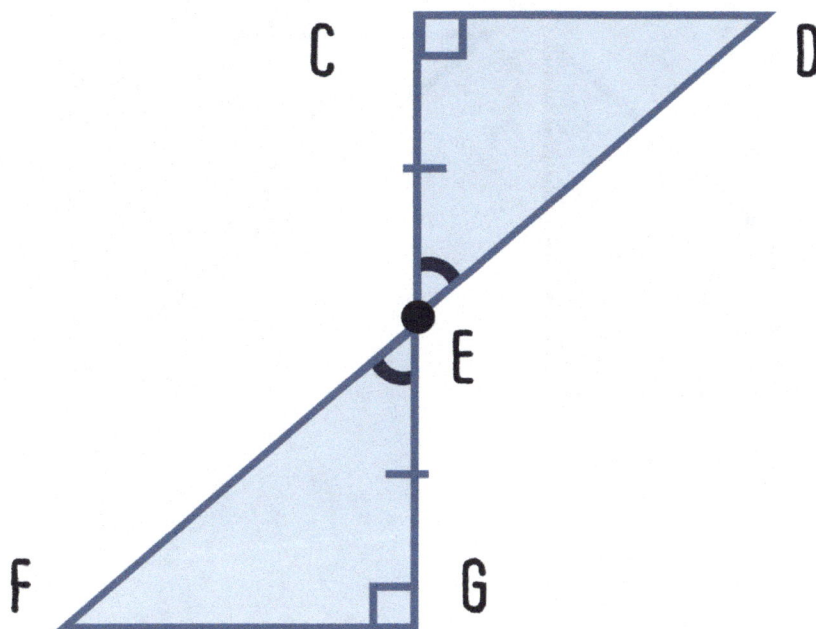

Hypotenuse Leg Congruence

If the hypotenuse and a leg of one right triangle is congruent to the hypotenuse and corresponding leg of another right triangle, then the triangles are congruent.

Geometry Crash Course   By Francesca Tamano

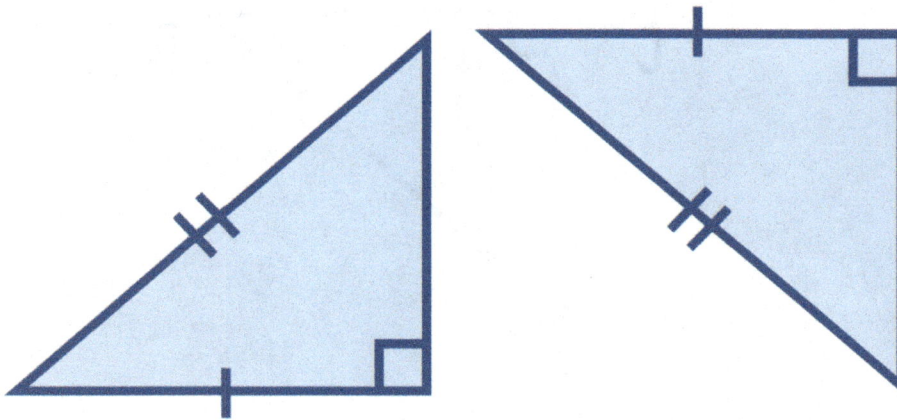

Isosceles and Equilateral Triangles

An isosceles triangle is a triangle with at least 2 sides congruent. The two congruent sides are called the legs of the isosceles triangle. The angle between the sides that are the legs is called the vertex angle of an isosceles triangle. The base is opposite the vertex angle and the 2 angles formed by the base and the congruent sides are called the base angles of an isosceles triangle.

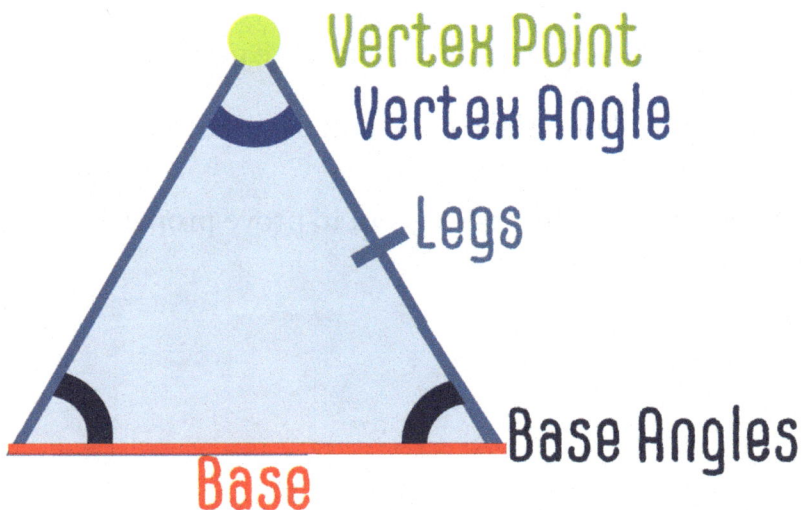

If two sides of a triangle are congruent, then the angles opposite those sides are congruent (the base angles are congruent)

If 2 angles of a triangle are congruent, then the sides opposite those 2 angles are congruent (the 2 legs are congruent to each other

Equilateral Triangles:

A triangle is equilateral if and only if it is equiangular (all angles = 60°)

Each angle of an equilateral triangle measures 60°

Triangles and Coordinate Proofs

Coordinates proofs use figures in the coordinate plane and algebra to prove geometric concepts. The first step in a coordinate proof is placing the figure on the coordinate plane. Make it as simple as necessary.

Then, determine the coordinates and use algebra to prove properties or theorems

Geometry Crash Course   By Francesca Tamano

Module 6: Relationships in Triangles

Perpendicular Bisectors

A perpendicular bisector is a line, segment, or ray that passes through the midpoint of the segment and is perpendicular to that segment.

If a point is on the perpendicular bisector of a segment, then it is equidistant from the endpoints of that segment.

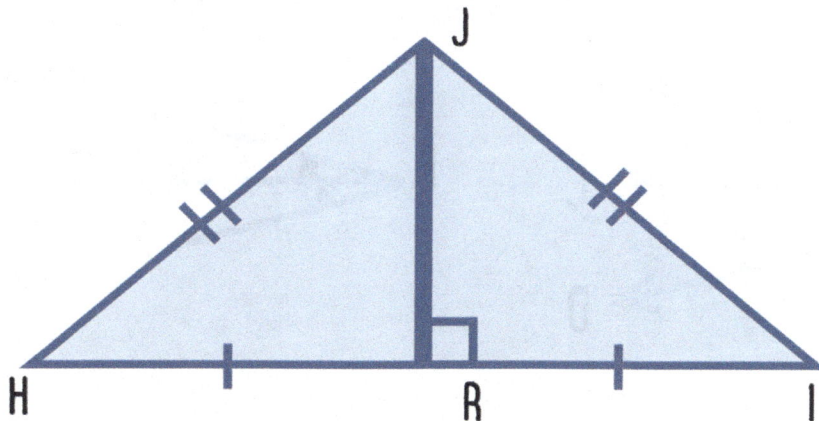

When 3 or more lines intersect at the same point, then those lines can be called concurrent lines.

The point of intersection can be called the point of concurrency.

The circumcenter of the triangle is where the triangle's perpendicular bisectors meet.

The perpendicular bisectors of a triangle intersect at a point called the circumcenter that is equidistant from the vertices of the triangle

Angle Bisectors

An angle bisector is a ray, line, or segment that divides an angle into 2 congruent angles.

If a point is on an angle bisector, then it is equidistant from the sides of that angle.

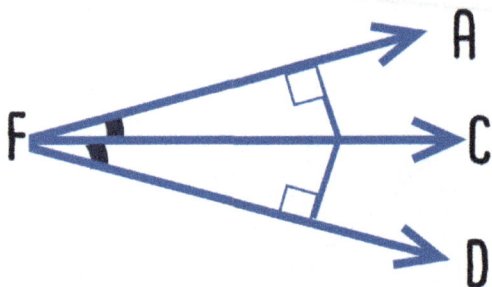

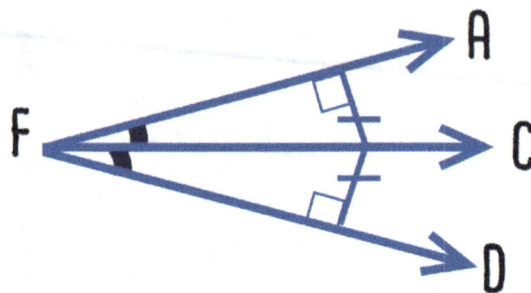

If a point in the interior of an angle is equidistant from the sides of the angle, then it is on the angle bisector

All triangles have 3 angle bisectors. The point of concurrency, or the point where the 3 angle bisectors meet, is the triangle's incenter.

The angle bisectors of a triangle at the ==incenter. The triangle's incenter is== ==equidistant from the triangle's sides.==

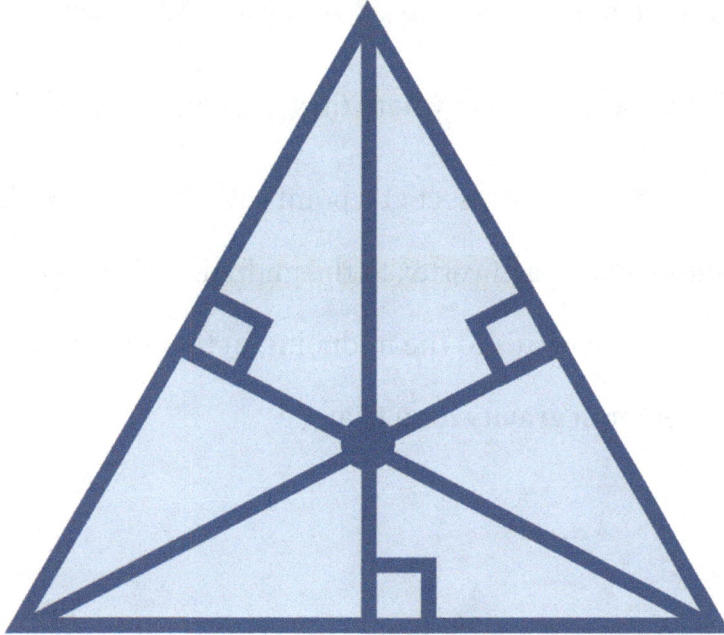

Medians and Altitudes of a Triangle

In a triangle, a median is a line segment with endpoints that are a vertex of the triangle and the midpoint of the side opposite the vertex.

Every triangle has medians, and where they intersect is called the centroid.

The medians of a triangle intersect at a point called the centroid, which is 2/3 of the distance from each vertex to the midpoint of the opposite side. (2/3 distance from the vertex to the midpoint, in that direction). The centroid is the center of gravity for a triangle.

The altitude of a triangle is a segment from a vertex of the triangle to the opposite side and is perpendicular to that side.

All triangles have altitudes. If extended, the altitudes intercept, the point of intersection is called the orthocenter.

Geometry Crash Course   By Francesca Tamano

Inequalities in One Triangle

Inequality Properties	
Let a, b, and c be real numbers	
Multiplication Property	If $a < b$ and $c > 0$, then $ac < bc$ If $a < b$ and $c < 0$, then $ac > bc$
Subtraction Property	If $a < b$, then $a - c < b - c$
Addition Property	If $a < b$, then $a + c < b + c$
Division Property	If $a < b$ and $c > 0$, then $\frac{a}{c} < \frac{b}{c}$ If $a < b$ and $c < 0$, then $\frac{a}{c} > \frac{b}{c}$
Comparison Property	If $a = b + c$ and $c > 0$, then $a > b$
Transitive Property	If $a < b$ and $a < c$, then $c < b$

Exterior Angle Inequality:

Geometry Crash Course   By Francesca Tamano

The measure of a triangle's exterior angle is always greater than the measure of either of that angle's remote interior angles.

Angle-Side Relationships in Triangles

If one side of a triangle is longer than another side, then the angle opposite the longer side has a greater measure than the angle opposite the shorter side.

If one angle of a triangle has a greater measure than another angle, then the side opposite the angle with the greater measure is longer than the side opposite the angle with the lesser measure.

Geometry Crash Course   By Francesca Tamano

Indirect Proofs

Indirect reasoning eliminates all possible conclusions but one, so the one remaining conclusion must be true. In an indirect proof, or proof by contradiction, one assumes that the statement that must be proven is false and uses logical reasoning to deduce that a statement contradicts a postulate, theorem, or one of the assumptions. Once a contradiction is obtained, the statement assumed false must be TRUE.

In indirect proofs, you should assume that the conclusion you are trying to prove is false. If in the proof, you prove that the hypothesis is false, then this is proof by contrapositive. If in the proof, you prove that some other fact is false, then this is proof by contradiction.

The Triangle Inequality

For 3 segments to form a triangle, a special relationship must exist among their lengths.

The sum of the lengths of any 2 sides of a triangle is greater than the length of the 3rd side.

a, b, c correspond to SIDES!

$$a + b > c$$

$$a + c > b$$

$$b + c > a$$

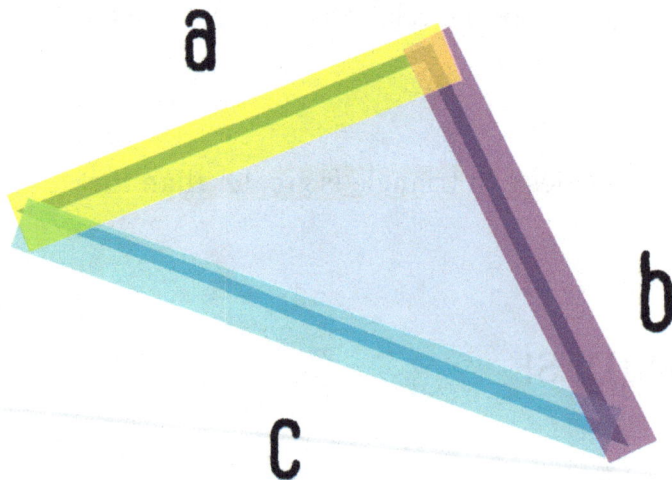

Here is how to find possible side lengths (using a range of values):

==Let X represent the length of a 3rd side of a triangle with sides that measure 8 miles and 4 miles.==

So, we set up some equations using the Triangle Inequality Theorem.

$8+4 > x$

$x+4 > 8$

$x+8 > 4$

Geometry Crash Course   By Francesca Tamano

Thus,

$$4 < x < 12$$

Inequalities in 2 Triangles

Hinge Theorem

If 2 sides of a triangle are congruent to 2 sides of another triangle, and the included angle of the 1st is larger than the included angle of the 2nd, the 3rd side of the 1st triangle is longer than the 3rd side of the second triangle.

Converse of the Hinge Theorem

If 2 sides in 2 triangles are congruent to each other, and the 3rd side of the 1st triangle is longer than the 3rd side of the 2nd triangle, then the included angle measure of the 1st triangle is greater than the included angle measure of the 2nd triangle

Module 7: Quadrilaterals

Angles of Polygons

==A diagonal of a polygon is a segment that connects any of the 2 nonconsecutive vertices within a polygon.== The sum of the ==angle measures of a polygon is the sum of the angle measures of the triangles formed by drawing all possible diagonals from one vertex.==

R and S are nonconsecutive to P. Since ==all triangles have an angle sum of 180, then 180 x 3 = the sum of the polygon's angle measures.==

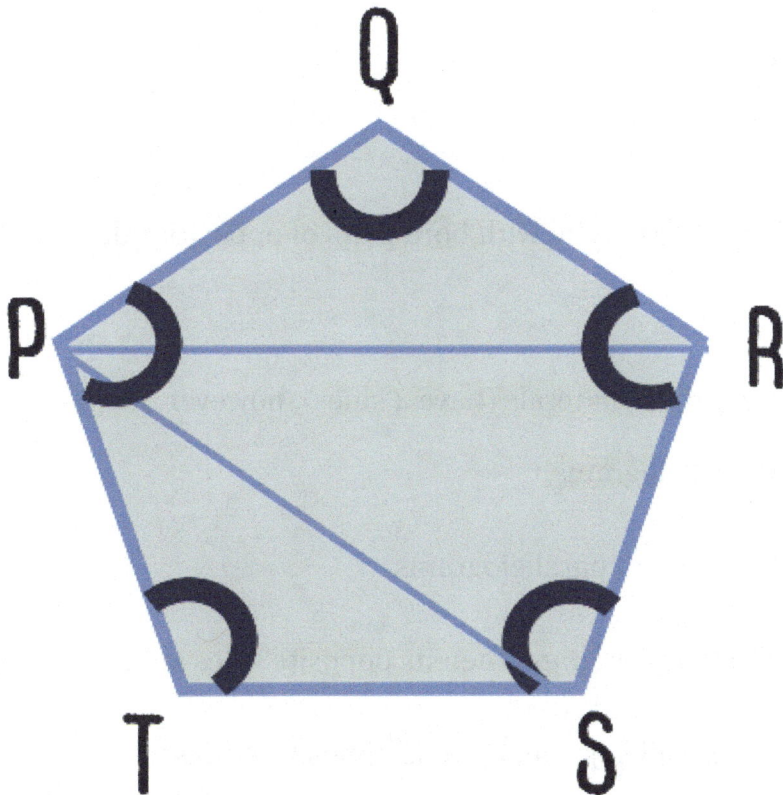

Using this proof, we can create this theorem.

Polygon Interior Angles Sum Theorem

The sum of the interior angle measures of an n-sided *convex* polygon is 180(n-2).

Polygon Exterior Angles Sum Theorem

The sum of the exterior angle measures of a convex polygon, one angle at each vertex, is 360°.

Parallelograms

A parallelogram is a quadrilateral with both pairs of opposite sides parallel.

All parallelograms are quadrilaterals (have 4 sides), however, not all quadrilaterals are parallelograms.

There are other properties of parallelograms.

If a quadrilateral is a parallelogram, then its opposite sides are congruent.

If a quadrilateral is a parallelogram, then its opposite angles are congruent.

If a quadrilateral is a parallelogram, then its consecutive angles are supplementary (add up to 180°)

If a parallelogram has 1 right angle, then it has 4 right angles.

The diagonals of parallelograms have special properties.

If a quadrilateral is a parallelogram, then its diagonals bisect each other.

If a quadrilateral is a parallelogram, then each diagonal separates the parallelogram into 2 congruent triangles.

Tests for Parallelograms

If a quadrilateral has 2 pairs of opposite sides parallel, it is a parallelogram. However, there are other tests for parallelograms.

If a quadrilateral has a pair of opposite sides parallel, it is a parallelogram.

If both pairs of opposite sides of a quadrilateral are congruent, then the quadrilateral is a parallelogram.

If both pairs of opposite angles of a quadrilateral are congruent, then the quadrilateral is a parallelogram.

If the diagonals of a quadrilateral bisect each other, then the quadrilateral is a parallelogram.

If one pair of opposite sides of a parallelogram is both parallel and congruent, then the quadrilateral is a parallelogram.

Rectangle

A rectangle is a parallelogram with 4 right angles.

All rectangles have the following properties:

- All right angles.

- Opposite sides are parallel and congruent.

- Consecutive angles are supplementary.

- Diagonals bisect each other.

If the diagonals of a parallelogram are congruent, then the parallelogram is a rectangle.

Geometry Crash Course   By Francesca Tamano

Rhombi and Squares

A rhombus is a parallelogram with all 4 sides congruent.

If a parallelogram is a rhombus, then its diagonals are perpendicular.

If a parallelogram is a rhombus, then each diagonal bisects a pair of opposite angles.

A square is a parallelogram with all 4 sides and 4 angles congruent. All the properties of parallelograms, rectangles, and rhombi apply to squares.

Tests for both Squares and Rhombi

If a parallelogram's diagonals are perpendicular, it is a rhombus.

If a diagonal of a parallelogram bisects opposite angles, then the parallelogram is a rhombus.

If 2 consecutive sides of a parallelogram are congruent, then the parallelogram is a rhombus.

If a quadrilateral is rhombus and a rhombus, then it is a square.

Trapezoids and Kites

A trapezoid is a quadrilateral with exactly 1 pair of parallel sides. The parallel sides are called bases of a trapezoid. The nonparallel sides are called the legs of a trapezoid. A base angle is formed by a trapezoid base and leg.

If the legs of the trapezoid are congruent, then it is an isosceles trapezoid.

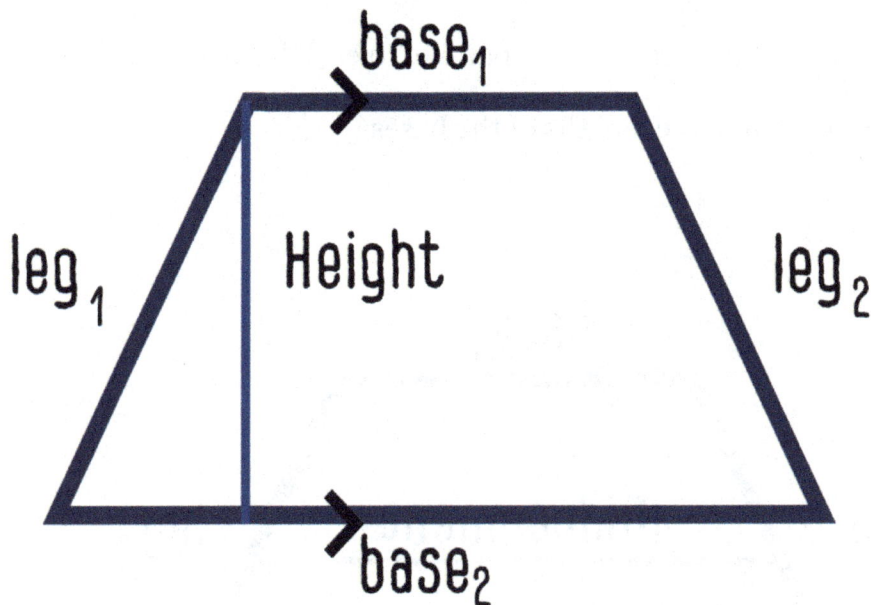

Isosceles Trapezoids

If a trapezoid is isosceles, then each pair of base angles is congruent.

If a trapezoid has one pair of congruent base angles, then it is an isosceles trapezoid.

A trapezoid is isosceles if and only if its diagonals are congruent.

The midsegment of a trapezoid is the segment that connects the midpoints of the legs of the trapezoid.

Trapezoid Midsegment:

The midsegment of a trapezoid is parallel to each base and its length is only half the sum of the lengths of the bases.

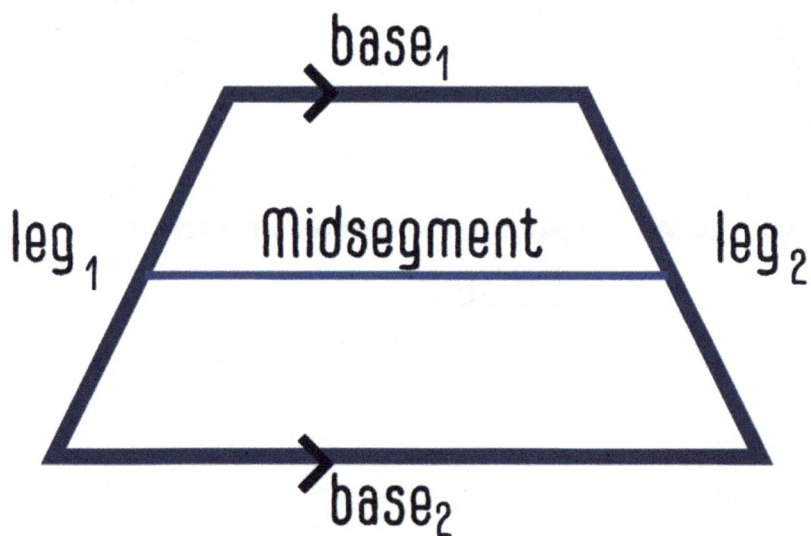

Kites:

A kite is a convex quadrilateral with exactly 2 distinct pairs of adjacent congruent sides.

If a quadrilateral is a kite, then its diagonals are perpendicular.

If a quadrilateral is a kite, then exactly 1 pair of opposite angles is congruent.

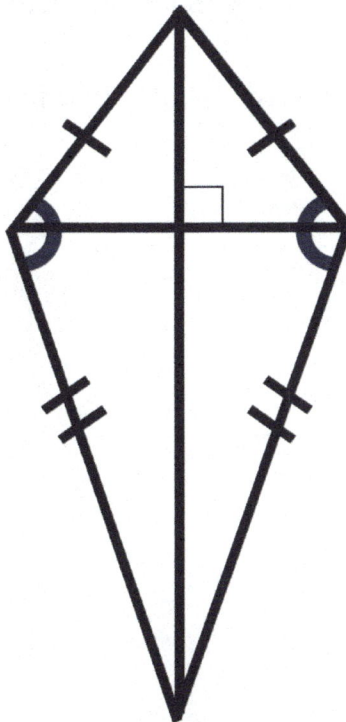

Geometry Crash Course   By Francesca Tamano

Module 8: Similarity

Dilations

Nonrigid transformation: changes the dimensions of a figure.

Dilation is a nonrigid transformation that reduces or enlarges a figure.

Center of dilation: the center through which dilations are performed. The scale factor of a dilation is the ratio of a length on an image to the preimage's corresponding length.

An enlargement is a dilation with a scale factor greater than 1

A reduction is a dilation with a scale factor between 0 and 1.

Geometry Crash Course   By Francesca Tamano

Similar Polygons

A dilation is a type of similarity transformation. A similarity

transformation is either a dilation or a composition of a dilation and rigid

transformations. ==Similar polygons if one can be obtained by the other with==

==a dilation or a composition of dilation and rigid transformations.==

Similar polygons

==2 polygons are similar if and only if they have congruent corresponding==

==angles and== proportional side lengths

There are reflexive, symmetric, and transitive properties of similarity

Perimeters of Similar Polygons:

==The ratio of any 2 corresponding quantities equals the scale factor of the==

==similarity ratio between them.==

Perimeters of Similar Polygons:

Geometry Crash Course   By Francesca Tamano

2 similar polygons will have perimeters that are proportional to the scale factor between them.

Similar Triangles

AA Similarity

==All the corresponding angles are congruent in similar triangles.== This means that all the corresponding angles have the same measures.

AA Similarity.

==If a triangle has 2 congruent angles with another triangle==, then the triangles are similar.

Similar Triangles SSS and SAS Similarity

SSS Similarity

Similar triangles will have proportional corresponding side lengths.

SAS Similarity

If the lengths of 2 sides of a triangle are proportional to the lengths of 2 corresponding sides of another triangle, and there are congruent included angles, then the triangles are similar.

Geometry Crash Course   By Francesca Tamano

Triangle Proportionality

When a triangle has a line that is parallel to one of its sides, the 2 triangles formed can be proven similar using AAA Similarity. If the triangles are similar, then their sides are proportional.

If a line intersects 2 sides but is parallel to the other side, then the line divides the sides into proportional segments.

If a line intersects 2 sides of a triangle, and separates the sides into proportional corresponding segments, then the line is parallel to the triangle's 3rd side.

The midsegment of a triangle is a segment that connects the midpoints of the legs of the triangle. There are 3 midsegments in every triangle.

A midsegment of a triangle is parallel to 1 of the triangle's sides, then the midsegment's length is 1 half of that side.

Proportional Parts of Parallel Lines

If 3 or more parallel lines intersect 2 transversals, then they cut off the transversal proportionally.

Congruent Parts of Parallel Line

If 3 or more parallel lines cut off congruent segments on 1 transversal, then they cut off congruent segments on every transversal

Geometry Crash Course   By Francesca Tamano

Geometry Crash Course   By Francesca Tamano

Parts of Similar Triangles

If 2 triangles are similar, then the lengths of the corresponding altitudes are proportional to the lengths of the corresponding sides.

If 2 triangles are similar, the lengths of the corresponding angle bisectors are proportional to the lengths of the corresponding sides

If 2 triangles are similar, the lengths of the corresponding medians are proportional to the lengths of the corresponding sides

An angle bisector in a triangle separates the opposite side into 2 segments that are proportional to the lengths of the other 2 sides

Geometry Crash Course   By Francesca Tamano

Module 9: Right Angles and Trigonometry

Pythagorean Theorem and its Converse

In a right triangle, the sum of the squares of the legs equals the square of

the hypotenuse.

A Pythagorean triple is a set of nonzero whole numbers A, B, and C, such as that

$a^2 + b^2 = c^2$ (hypotenuse)

Common Pythagorean Triples:

7, 24, 25	9, 40, 41	11, 60, 61	3, 4, 5	5, 12, 13	8, 1
14, 48, 50	18, 80, 82	22, 120, 122	6, 8, 10	10, 24, 26	16,
21, 72, 75	27, 120, 123	33, 180, 183	9, 12, 15	15, 36, 39	24,
28, 96, 100	36, 160, 164	44, 240, 244	12, 16, 20	20, 48, 52	32,
35, 120, 125	45, 200, 205	55, 300, 305	15, 20, 25	25, 60, 65	40,

Converse of the Pythagorean Theorem

If the sum of the squares of the lengths of the shortest sides of a triangle is

equal to the square of the longest side, then the triangle is a right triangle

If the square of the longest side of a triangle is less than the sum of the

squares of the other 2 sides, the triangle is acute

If the square of the longest side of the triangle is greater than the squares

of the lengths of the other 2 sides, then the triangle is obtuse.

Geometry Crash Course   By Francesca Tamano

Special Right Triangles

The diagonal of a square forms 2 congruent isosceles right triangles

In a 45 -45 -90 triangle, the legs are congruent, and the length of the hypotenuse is square root of 2 times the leg.

When an altitude in an equilateral triangle is formed, 2 congruent 30-60-90 triangles are formed.

In a 30-60-90 triangle, the length of the hypotenuse is the length of the longest leg multiplied by 2. The longest leg is the square root of the shortest leg multiplied by 3.

Trigonometry

A trigonometric ratio is the ratio of 2 sides of a right triangle.

SOH CAH TOA

Trigonometric Ratio

Sine: if Triangle ABC is a right triangle, then the sine of each acute angle in ABC has the ratio of the lengths of the leg opposite that angle to the length of the hypotenuse.

Cosine: If Triangle AB is a right triangle, the cosine of each acute angle in ABC is the ratio of the length of the leg nearby that angle to the length of the hypotenuse

Tangent: If Triangle ABC is a right triangle, then the tangent of each acute angle in ABC is the ratio of the leg opposite that angle to the length of the leg adjacent that angle.

Inverse Trigonometric Ratios:

Inverse sine: If ∠A is an acute angle, and the sine of A is x, then the inverse sine of x is the measure of ∠A

Inverse cosine: If ∠A is acute and the cosine of A is x, then the inverse cosine of x is the measure of ∠A.

Inverse tangent: If ∠A is an acute angle, and the tangent of A is x, then the

inverse tangent of x is the measure of ∠A

Applying Trigonometry

You can measure something through indirect measurement, which involves using similar figures and proportions to measure an object.

Angle of elevation: formed by horizontal line and line above horizontal line

Angle of depression: formed by horizontal line and line below the horizontal line

Angles of elevation and depression are always formed with a horizontal line, never with a vertical line

Trigonometry and Areas of Triangles

One formula for the area of a triangle, A = ½ bh

When the height is unknown, then the triangle's area is found using

Area = ½ absinc where a and b are side lengths and C is the included

angle.

The Law of Sines

If triangle ABC has lengths a, b, and c, representing the sides opposite

angles A, B, and C, then

$$\frac{a}{sinA} = \frac{b}{sinB} = \frac{c}{sinC}$$

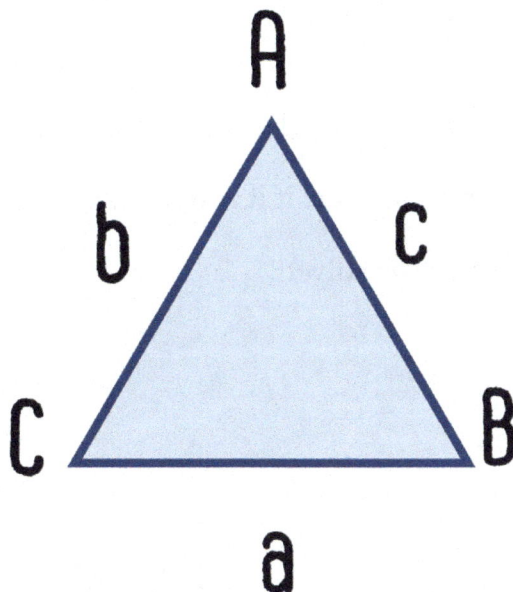

It can be used with 2 angles of a triangle and one non included side.

In addition, A°+B°+C°= 180°

When given AAS, or the measures of 2 angles and 1 side, exactly 1 triangle is possible. However, if you are given the measures of 2 sides and the angle opposite one of them, SSA, zero, one, or two solutions (triangles) may be possible.

The sine of an obtuse angle is defined to be the sine of its supplement. x = sin (180-the obtuse angle)

Once you find the measure of 1 angle, subtract it from 180. Add the new amount to the given angle and see if it is less than 180. If it is, then you have 2 triangles that must be solved.

Geometry Crash Course   By Francesca Tamano

The Law of Cosines

When the law of Sines cannot solve a triangle, you can use the law of cosines.

The Law of Cosines is used to find the length of the 3rd side of a triangle when the measures of the 2 sides and the included angle are known. In addition, the Law of Cosines can be used to find the angle measures of a triangle if the lengths of all 3 sides are known.

Law of Cosines

If triangle ABC has lengths a, b, and c, representing the lengths of the sides opposite angles with the measures A, B, and C, then.

$$a^2 = b^2 + c^2 - 2bc\ \cos(A)$$

$$b^2 = a^2 + c^2 - 2ac\ \cos(B)$$

$$c^2 = a^2 + b^2 - 2ab\ \cos(C)$$

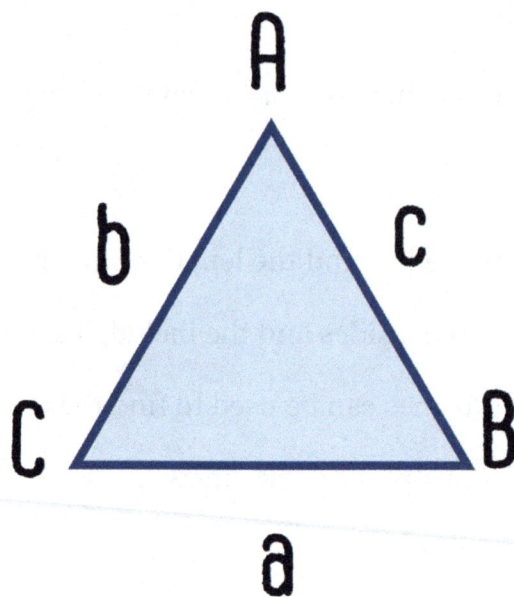

Module 10: Circles

Circles and Circumference

A circle is the set of all points in a plane that are equidistant from the center of a circle.

The radius of a circle is a line segment from the center to a point on the circle.

A chord of a circle is a segment with endpoints on the circle.

A diameter is a chord that passes through the center of a circle.

Two circles are congruent if and only if they have congruent radii

All circles are similar

Measuring Angles and Arcs

A central angle of a circle is an angle with a vertex at the center of a circle and sides that are radii.

A degree is 1/360 of a circular rotation about a point.

The sum of the measures of the central angles is 360°.

An arc is a part of a circle that is defined by 2 endpoints. A central angle separates the circle into 2 arcs with measures related to the measure of the central angle.

Minor arc = less than 180°

Major arc= more than 180°

Semicircle = exactly 180°

Congruent arcs are arcs in congruent circles that have the same measure

In the same circle or in congruent circles, 2 minor arcs are congruent if and only if their central angles are congruent.

The measure of an arc formed by 2 adjacent arcs is the sum of the measures of the 2 arcs

Arc Length and Radian Measure:

An intercepted arc is the part of the circle that lies between the 2 lines intercepting it.

Arc length is the distance between the endpoints of an arc that is measured along the arc in linear units.

Arc length = proportional to radius.

Arcs and Chords

A chord is a segment with endpoints on a circle. If a chord is not a diameter, then its endpoints divide the circle into a major and minor arc.

In the same circle or congruent circles, 2 minor arcs are congruent if and only if their corresponding chords are congruent.

If a diameter or radius of a circle is perpendicular to a chord, then it bisects the chord and its arc.

The perpendicular bisector of a chord contains a diameter or radius of a circle.

In the same circle, or in congruent circles, chords are congruent if and only if they are equidistant from the center.

Inscribed Angles

An inscribed angle is an angle that has its vertex on a circle and sides that contain chords of the circle.

Inscribed Angle Theorem:

If an angle is inscribed in a circle, then the measure of its angle equals ½ the measure of its intercepted arc.

If 2 inscribed angles of a circle intercept congruent arcs or the same arc, then the pair of angles are congruent.

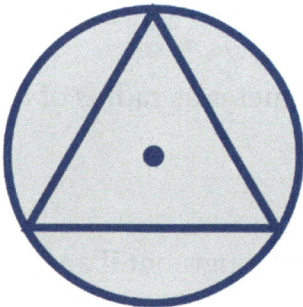

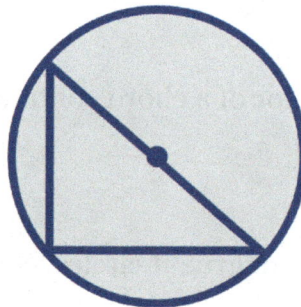

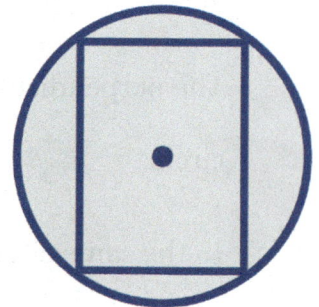

Inscribed Polygons:

In an inscribed polygon, all the vertices of the polygon lie on a circle.

An inscribed angle of a triangle intercepts a diameter or semicircle if and only if the angle is a right angle.

If a quadrilateral is inscribed in a circle, then its opposite angles are supplementary.

The circumscribed circle of a polygon is the circle that contains all the vertices of the polygon. The circumcenter of a triangle is the center of the circumscribed circle.

Circumcenter of a triangle:	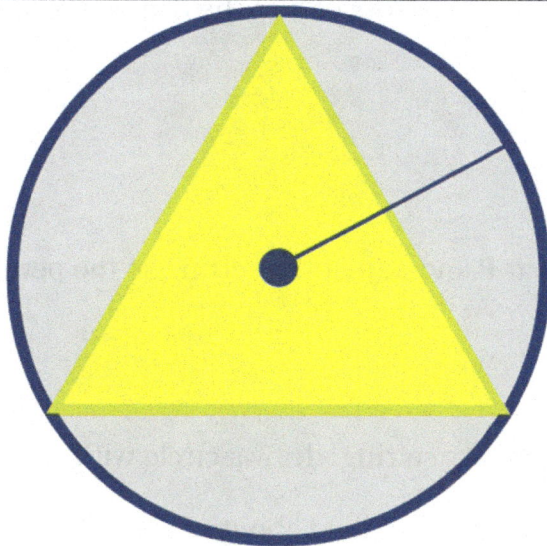

Incenter of the triangle:	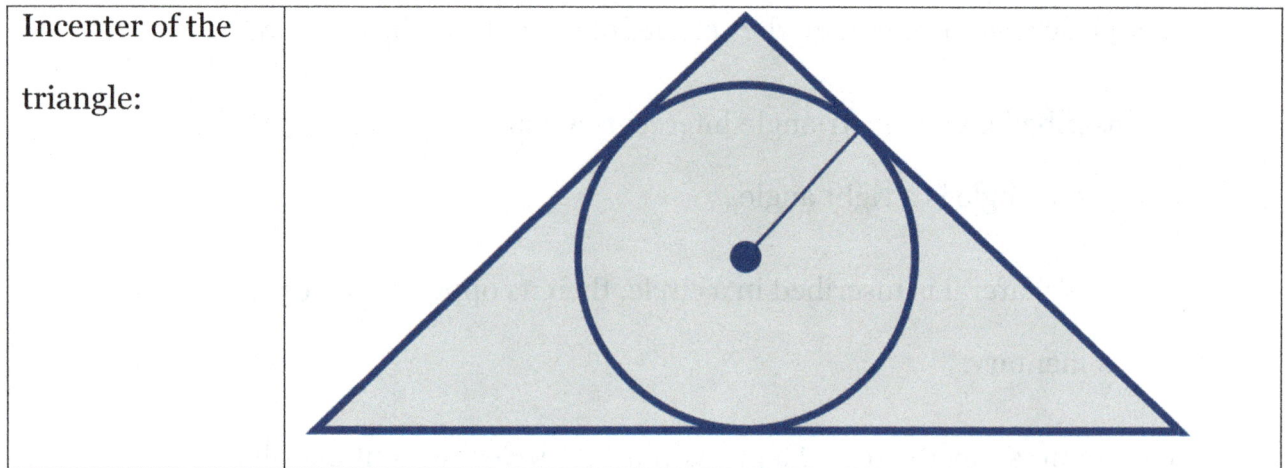

Steps to Constructing the Circumscribed Circle of a Triangle

Step 1:

Construct the perpendicular bisectors of 2 of the triangle ABC sides. Label their circumcenter point P.

Step 2:

Place the compass point at P and adjust the setting so the pencil is at A.

Step 3:

Without changing the compass setting, draw a circle with center P and radius AP. Circle P is now circumscribed about triangle ABC.

Geometry Crash Course   By Francesca Tamano

Tangents

A tangent to a circle is a line or segment in the plane of the circle that intersects the circle at precisely 1 point and does not contain any points in the interior of the circle.

For a line that intersects the circle in 1 point, the point of tangency is where they intersect.

A common tangent is a line or segment that is tangent to 2 circles in the same plane.

In a plane, a line is tangent to a circle if and only if it is perpendicular to a radius drawn to the point of tangency.

Tangent to a Circle Theorem:

If 2 segments from the same exterior point are tangent to a circle, then they are congruent

A circumscribed angle is an angle with sides that are tangent to a circle.

If 2 segments or lines are tangent to a circle, then the circumscribed angle and the central angle that intercept the arc formed by the points of tangency are supplementary,

Geometry Crash Course   By Francesca Tamano

A circumscribed polygon has vertices outside the circle and sides that are tangent to the circle.

An inscribed circle is a circle in the interior of a polygon that intersects each side of the polygon at a single point.

How to make an Inscribed Circle of a Triangle:

Step 1:

Draw triangle ABC. Construct the angle bisectors of the 3 angles. Label the incenter D.

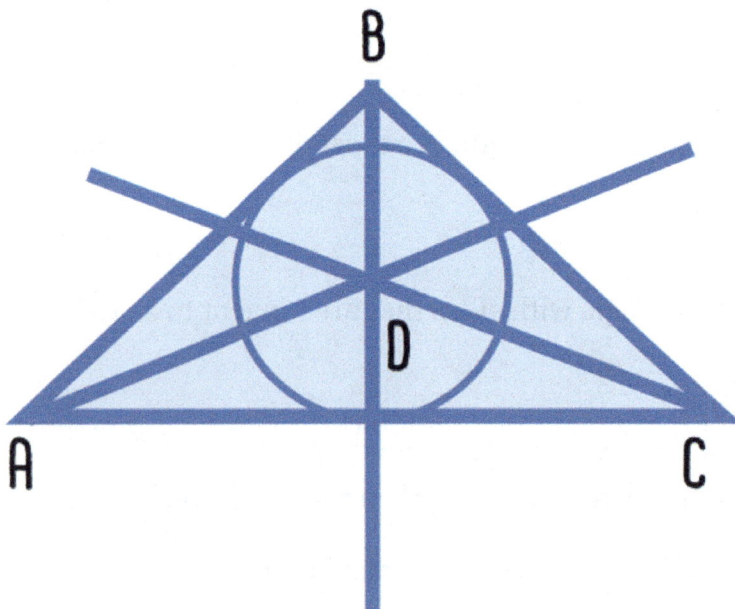

Step 2:

Construct a line perpendicular to AC that goes through D. Label the point

of the intersection of the perpendicular line as E.

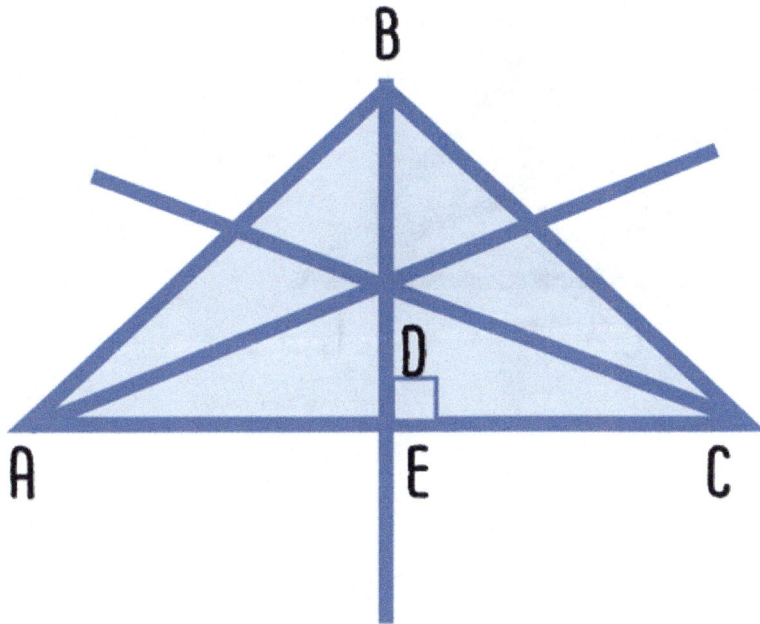

Step 3:

Construct the radius DE. Construct the inscribed circle using center D and

radius DE. If possible, hide unnecessary lines.

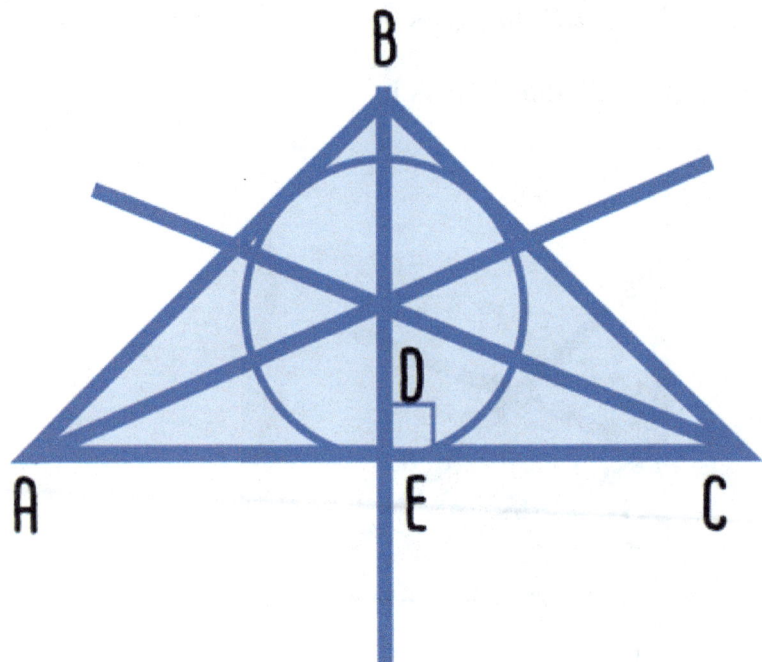

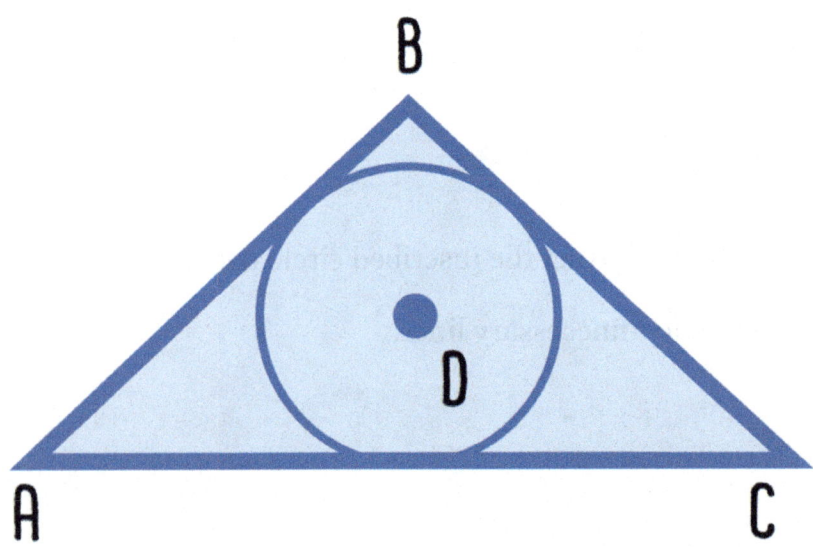

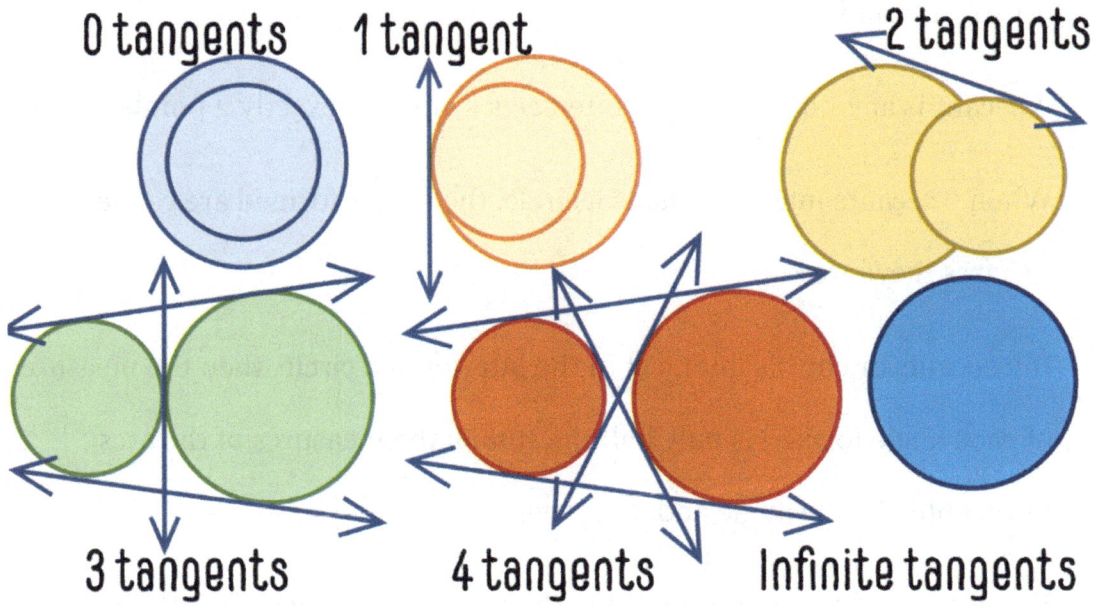

3 Tangents and Scants

A secant is any line or ray that intersects a circle in exactly 2 points.

When 2 secants intersect inside a circle, the angles formed are related to the arcs they intercept.

If 2 secants or chords intersect in the interior of a circle, then the measure of each angle formed is only half the sum of the measures of the arcs intercepted by the angle and its vertical angle.

If a secant and tangent intersect at the point of tangency, then the measure of each angle formed is ½ the measure of its intercepted arc.

If 2 secants, a secant, and a tangent, or 2 tangents intersect in the exterior of a Circle, then the measures of the angle formed is one half the difference between the measures of the intercepted arcs.

When 2 chords intersect inside a circle, each chord is divided into chord segments. A secant segment is a segment of a secant line that has exactly one endpoint on the circle. An external secant segment is a secant segment that lies in the exterior of the circle. A tangent segment is the segment of a tangent with one endpoint on the circle.

If 2 chords intersect in a circle, then the products of the lengths of the chord segments are equal.

If 2 secants intersect in the exterior of a circle, then the product of the measures of one secant segment and its external segment is equal to the product of the measures of the other secant segment and its external secant segment/

$R(Q+R) = S(T+S)$

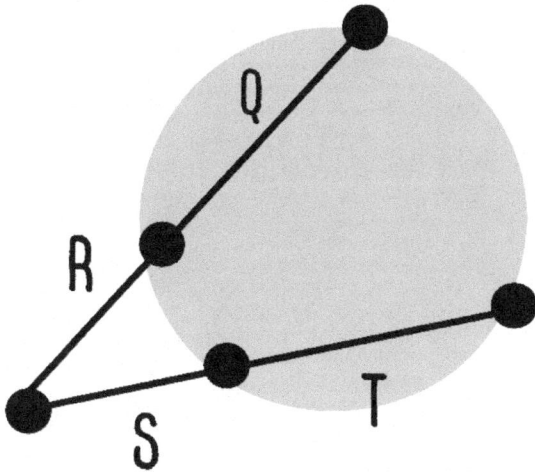

Secant Tangent Rule

If a tangent and secant intersect in the exterior of a circle, then the square of the measure of the tangent is equal to the product of the measures of the secant and its external secant segment.

$$AQ \cdot AR = AS^2$$

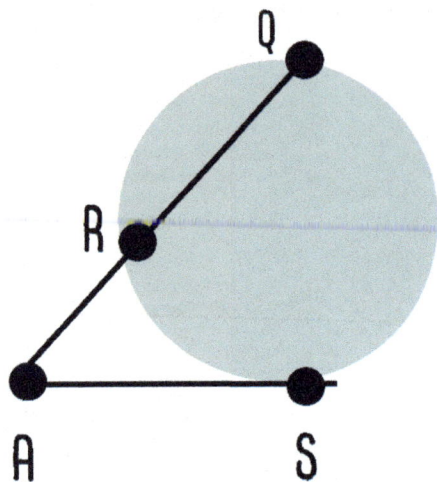

Equations of Circles

Because all points on a circle are equidistant from the center.

This is the standard form for the equation of a circle, with center (h, k)

$$(x - h)^2 + (y - k)^2 = r^2$$

Example:

The circle has a center of (3, 3) and the radius is 3.

$$(x - 3)^2 + (y - 3)^2 = 9$$

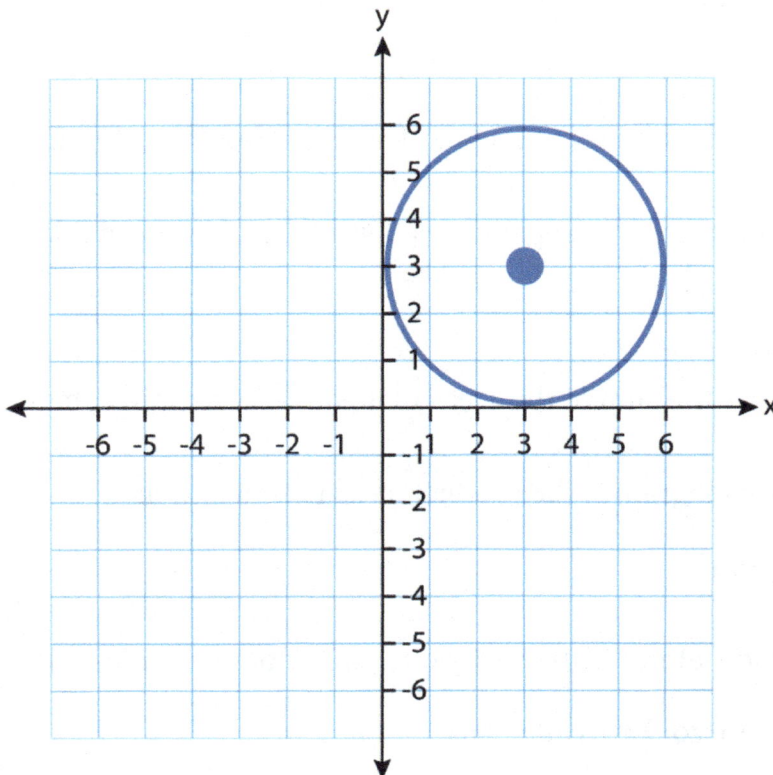

Module 11: Geometric Measurement

Areas of Quadrilaterals

A parallelogram is a quadrilateral in which both pairs of opposite sides are parallel.

The base of a parallelogram is on any side of the parallelogram.

The altitude of a parallelogram is a perpendicular segment between any 2 parallel bases.

The height of a parallelogram is the length of an altitude of a polygon.

Decomposition is the process of separating a figure into 2 or more non-overlapping parts.

The area of a region is the sum of the areas of its non-overlapping parts.

The area A of a parallelogram is the product of its base B and its corresponding height H.

A trapezoid is a quadrilateral with exactly one pair of parallel sides. The parallel sides of a trapezoid are called bases.

The height of a trapezoid is the perpendicular distance between the bases

of a trapezoid.

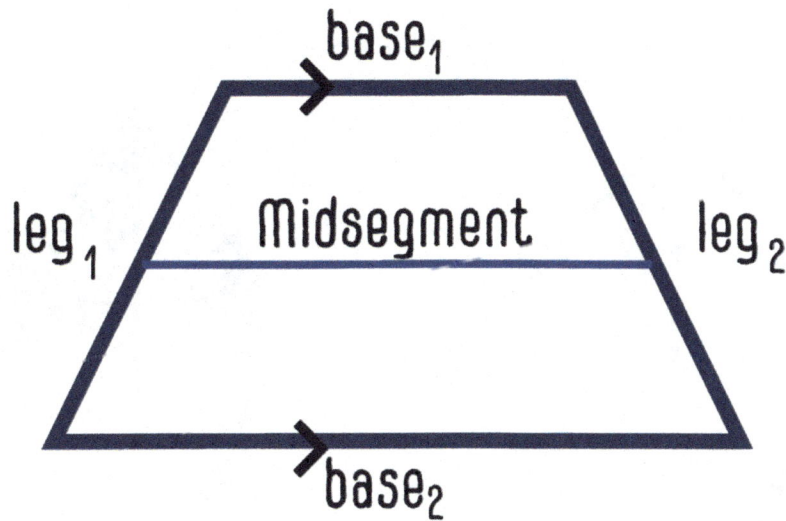

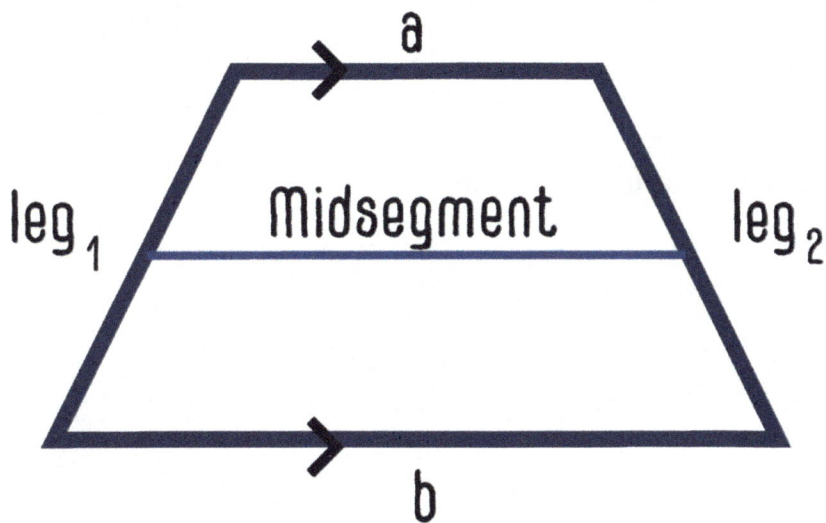

Area of a trapezoid:

$$\frac{1}{2}(a + b)\,h$$

A rhombus is a parallelogram with all 4 sides congruent, and a kite is a quadrilateral with exactly 2 pairs of consecutive congruent sides.

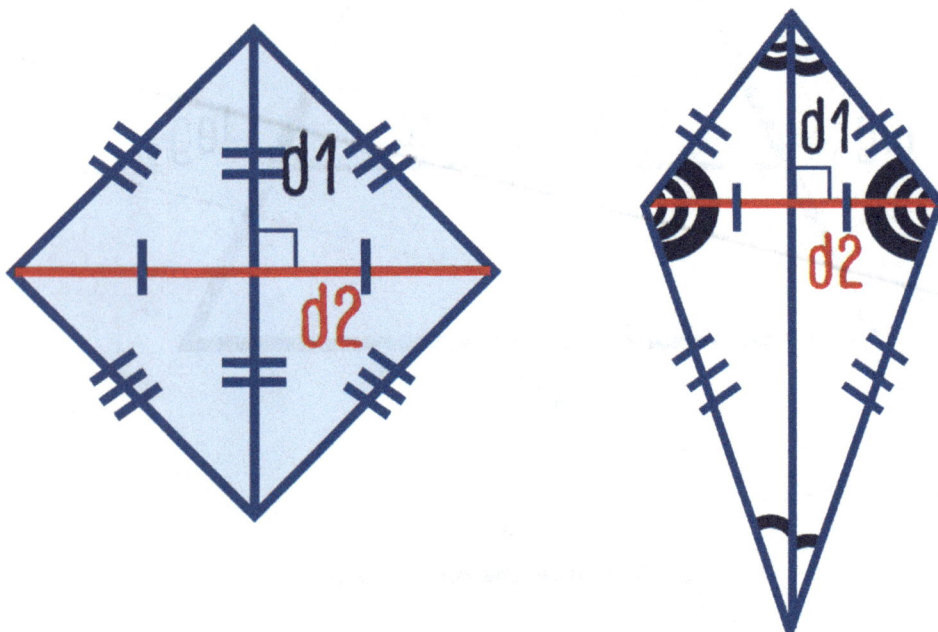

The rhombus and kite area formula is:

$$\frac{1}{2}d_1 d_2$$

Geometry Crash Course   By Francesca Tamano

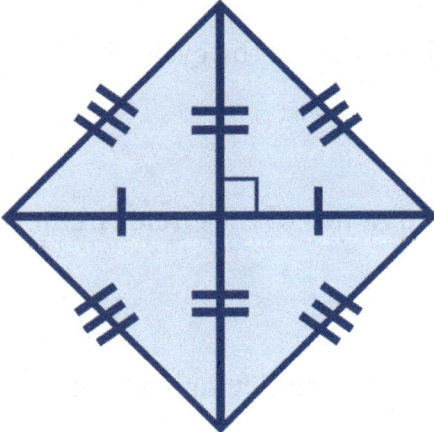

6 Areas of Regular Polygons

The center of a regular polygon is the center of the cycle circumscribed around the polygon.

The radius of a regular polygon is the radius of the circle circumscribed around the polygon.

The apothem of a regular polygon is a perpendicular segment between the center of the polygon and a side of the polygon.

The central angle of a regular polygon has its vertex at the center of the polygon and sides that pass through consecutive vertices of the polygon. The measure of each central angle of a regular n-gun is 360/n.

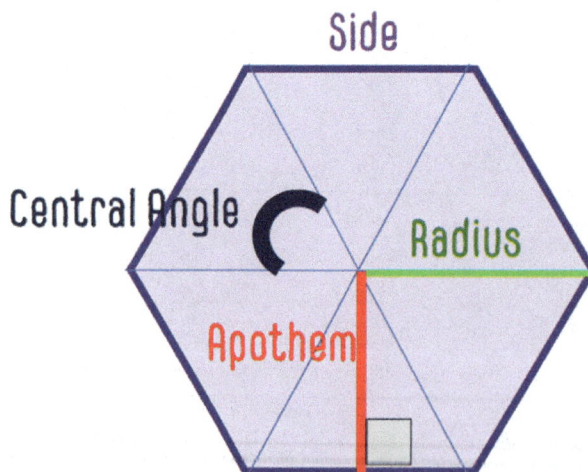

You can find the area of any regular n—gon by dividing the polygon into identical isosceles triangles. Find the area of 1 triangle and multiply that area by the total number of triangles.

The area of a triangle is ½ bh. The base of a triangle in a regular polygon is the length S of one side and the height of the triangle is the length of apothem A.

P = perimeter

Area of a polygon = ½ (a P)

A composite figure is a figure that can be separated into regions that are basic figures, such as triangles, rectangles, etc. To find the area of a compositive figure, find the area of each shape and add them together.

Geometry Crash Course   By Francesca Tamano

Areas of Circles and Sectors

The formula for the circumference C of a circle with radius r is given by C= 2πr.

Area of a circle: πr^2

A sector is a region of a circle bounded by a central angle and its intercepted arc.

Equation for sector area= $(\theta/360°)\, \pi r^2$

θ is the angle

Geometry Crash Course   By Francesca Tamano

Surface Area

The lateral area of a solid is the sum of the areas of the lateral faces of the solid. The lateral faces of a prism are the faces that join the bases of the prism. The lateral surface of a cylinder is the curved surface that joins the bases of the cylinder. The altitude of a prism or cylinder is the segment perpendicular to the bases that joins the planes of the bases. The height of a solid is the length of the altitude.

Lateral Area and Surface Area of a Right Prism

The lateral area is L of a right prism is L = Ph, where h is the height of the prism and P is the perimeter of the base.

The surface area S of the right prism is S = L + 2B, where L is the lateral area and B is the area of the base.

Right Cylinder:

Lateral Area: $2\pi rh$

Surface Area: L + 2B or s = $2\pi rh + 2\pi r^2$

A regular pyramid is a pyramid with a base that is a regular polygon. The lateral faces of a pyramid are the faces that join the base of the pyramid to the vertex. The lateral surface of a cone is the curved surface that joins the base to the vertex.

The height of a pyramid / cone is the length of the altitude of that shape.

L = slant height

P = perimeter of the base

Lateral Area of a Regular Pyramid:

$(½)Pl$

The Lateral Area of a Right Cones:

πrl

Surface Area of a Regular Pyramid:

S= L+B or S= $(½)Pl$ +B

Surface Area of a Right Cone:

S=L+B or S=πrl + πr^2

Surface Area of a Sphere:

$4\pi r^2$

Cross Sections and Solids of Revolution

A cross-section is the intersection of a solid figure and a plane. The shape of the cross-section formed by the intersection of the plane and the figure depends on the angle of the plane.

A 3-D figure has plane symmetry if the figure can be mapped onto itself by a reflection in the plane.

A solid revolution is a solid figure obtained by revolving a plane figure or curve around an axis.

A 3-D figure has axis symmetry if the figure can be mapped onto its leg by a rotation between 0 and 360.

Volumes of Prisms and Pyramids

Volume of a Prism: Bh

Cavalieri's Principle:

If 2 solids have the same height h and the same cross-sectional area B at every level, then they have the same volume.

The volume of a Pyramid:

The volume of a pyramid is: $\frac{1}{3}bh$.

Volumes of Cylinders, Cones, and Spheres

Volume of a Cylinder

$V = bh$ OR $v = \pi r^2 h$

You can use the Cavalieri's Principle to find the volumes of oblique

cylinders (slanted cylinders)

Volume of Cones:

$V = 1/3\ bh$

OR

$V = 1/3\ \pi r^2 h$

Volume of a Sphere: πr^3

$V = 4/3\ r^3$

Applying Similarity to Solid Figures

If 2 polygons are similar, then their perimeters are proportional to the scale factor between them.

If 2 polygons are similar, then their areas are proportional to the square of the scale factor.

Similar solids have different sizes but the same shape.

Similar solids: 2 solids are similar if they have the same shape, and the ratios of their corresponding linear measures are equal.

If 2 similar solids have a scale factor of a: b, then the surface areas have a ratio of $a^2: b^2$, and t the volumes have a ratio of a^3, b^3

Congruent solids:

Volumes are identical

Corresponding angles are congruent

Corresponding edges are congruent

Corresponding faces are congruent

Geometry Crash Course   By Francesca Tamano

Density

Density is a measure of the quantity of some physical property per unit of

length, area, or volume.

Density based on area = number of objects / areas

Density based on volume = mass or weight / volume

Practice Questions (No <mark>Graphing</mark> Calculator Required)

1. If Triangle ABC has angle C measuring 62° and angle B measuring 84°, then what is the measure of angle A?

2. A segment has a midpoint of (7, 4). One endpoint is (-14, 15). What is the other endpoint?

3. If angle A has a measure of 60°, then what is the measure of angle B?

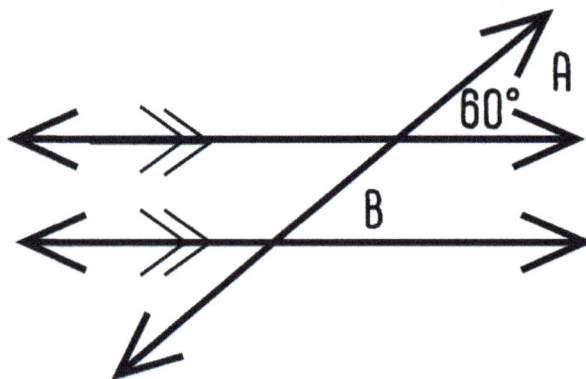

4. If angle C has a measure of 70°, then what is the measure of angle

    D?

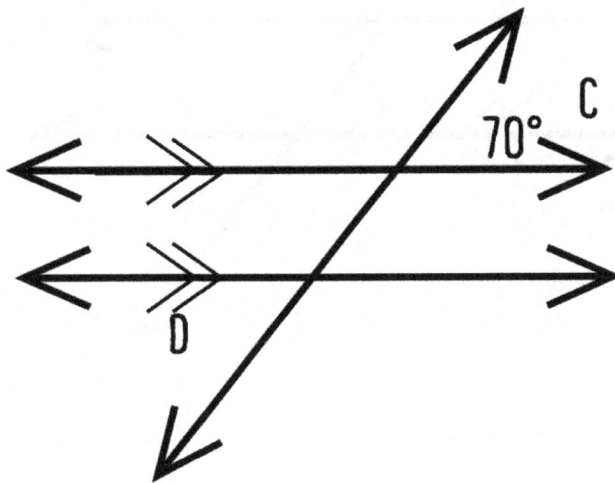

5. If the measure of angle S is 138°, then what is the measure of angle

    T?

138° S

T

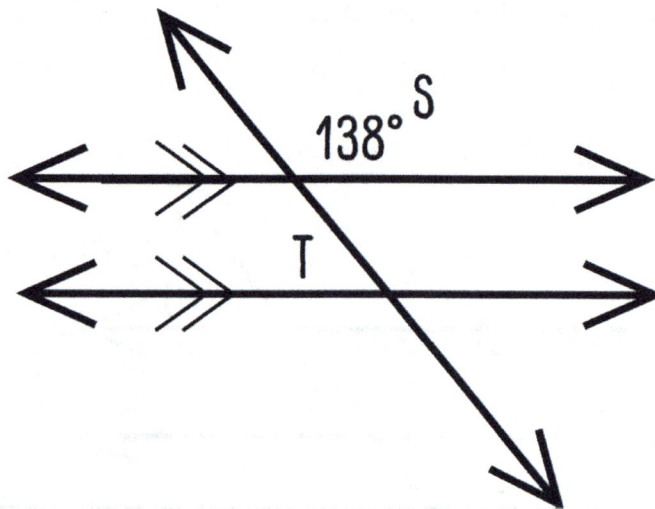

6. What is the measurement of angle A?

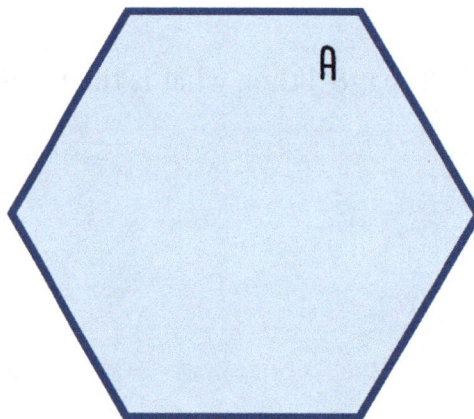

A

7. What is the measurement of segment CJ?

C   7

24

J

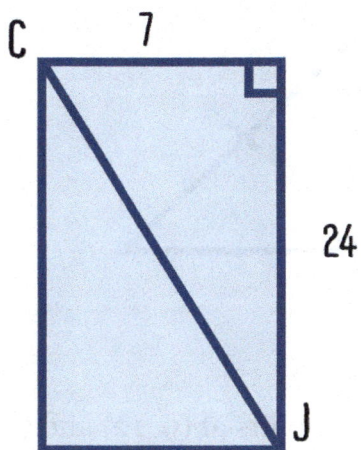

8. What is the midpoint of segment KT?

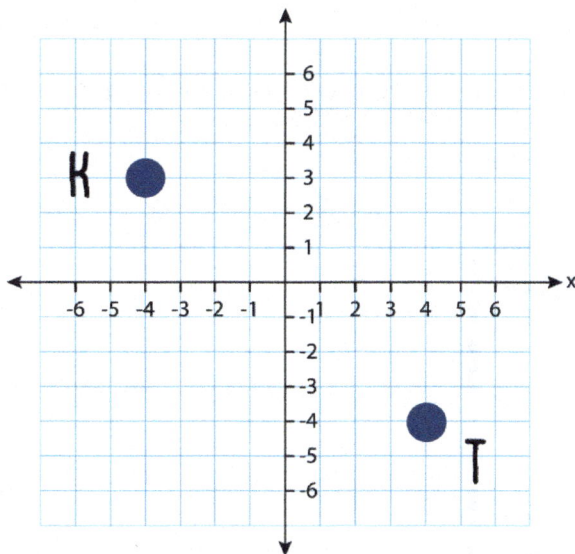

K ●

T

9. What type of triangle is shown?

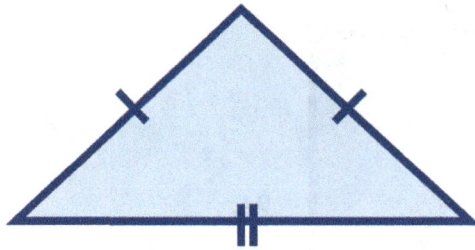

10. Segment AB has endpoints at (9, 12) and (36, 32). What is the

    length of segment AB, rounded to the nearest whole number?

11. What is the surface area, rounded to the nearest whole number, of

    the figure below?

20 cm

8cm

12. $x^2 - 8x + y^2 - 16y = -64$

What are the coordinates of the center? What is the length of the

radius?

13. Draw the circumscribed circle in the triangle shown below.

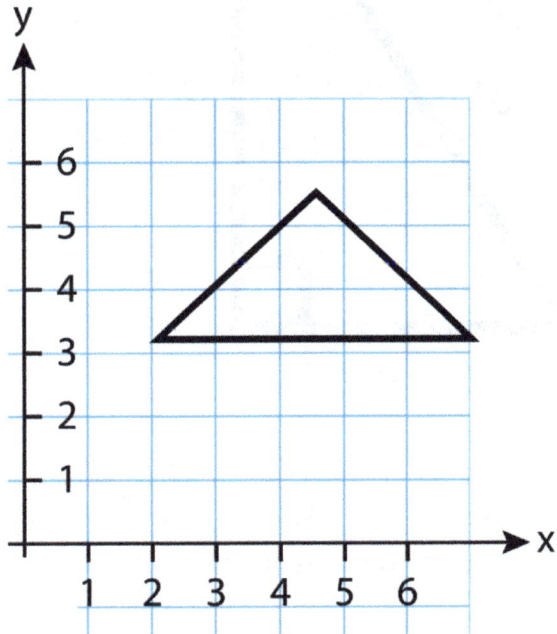

14. A figure has a volume of 3 cubic centimeters and a mass of 25 grams. What is its density per cubic centimeter, rounded to the nearest whole number?

15. What is the ratio Cosine (θ)?

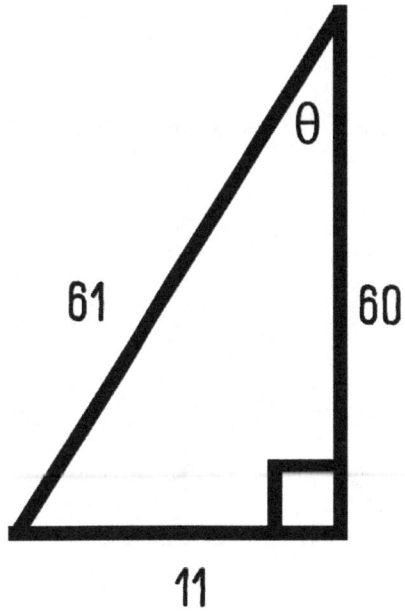

16. What theorem can be used to prove the two triangles congruent?

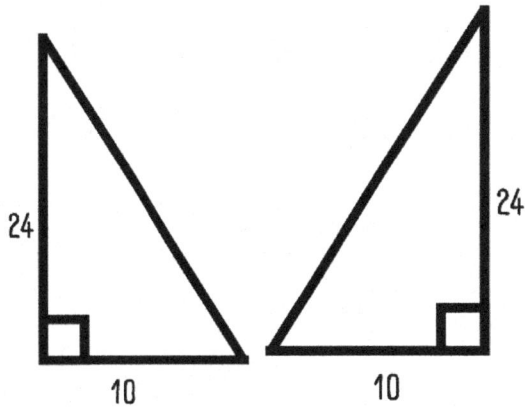

17. What is segment EF?

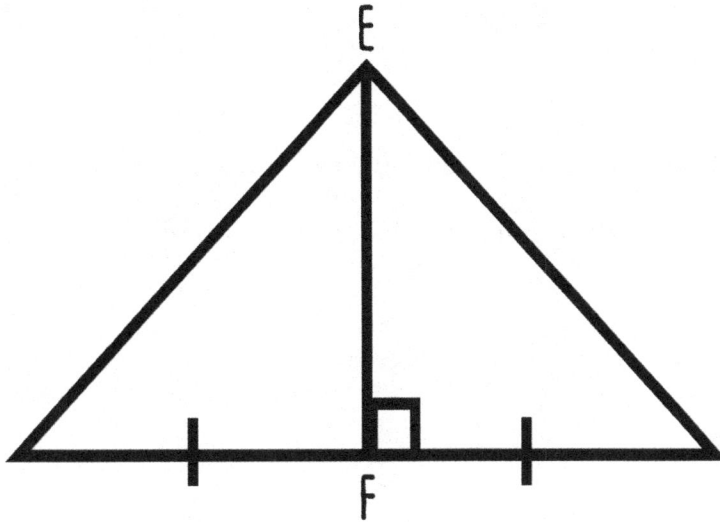

18. What is the converse of: "If Bob is at school, then Bob is wearing his uniform."

19. What is the measure of x?

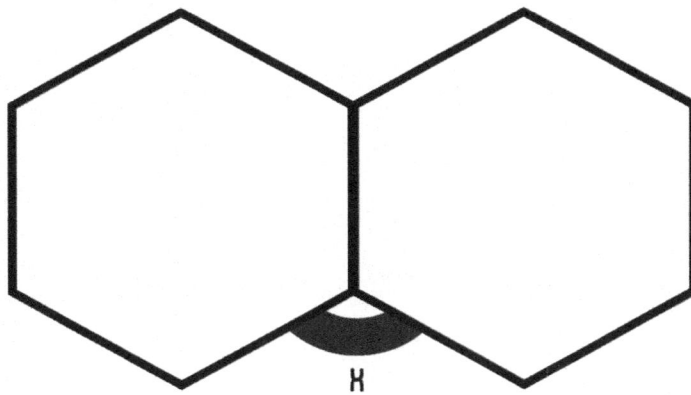

20.

Part A

A circle has radius N. It has tangent points H and K on the circle.

The radius is 30. What is the length of segment NH?

Part B

Segment HM and KM are tangent to the circle. *HM* = 40. What is

the Length of MN?

21. What is the area of the figure below?

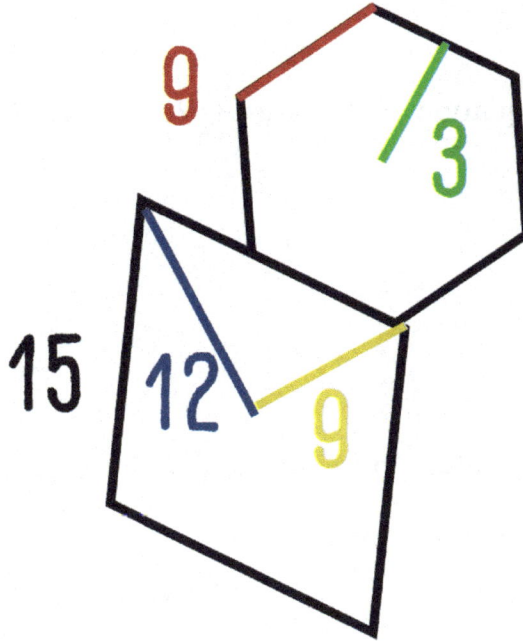

22. A circle has a diameter with endpoints (32, 80) and (24, 96). What is the circle's equation?

23. Part A: Point W is Point A (8, 9) translated by a vector of (8, 4). What are the coordinates of Point W?

Part B: What is the distance between Point A and Point W?

24. A circle has the equation $x^2 + y^2 - 8x + 20y = 10$. What is the circle's equation?

25. A cone has a height of 8 centimeters and a radius of 4 centimeters. What is the volume of the cone?

26. Sphere A has a radius of 6 centimeters. Sphere B has a radius of 2 centimeters. What is the difference in volume between Sphere A and Sphere B?

27. What is the measurement of arc YZX rounded to the nearest whole number?

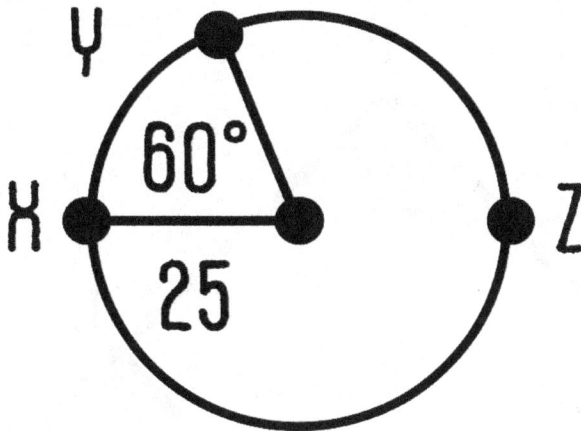

28. A cube has a volume of 3375 in^3. What is the cube's surface area?

29. If a 1 foot tall pole has a 3 foot long shadow, and a building has an 18 foot shadow, then how tall is the building?

30. Triangle TUV is similar to Triangle MLV. What is the measurement of angle LMV?

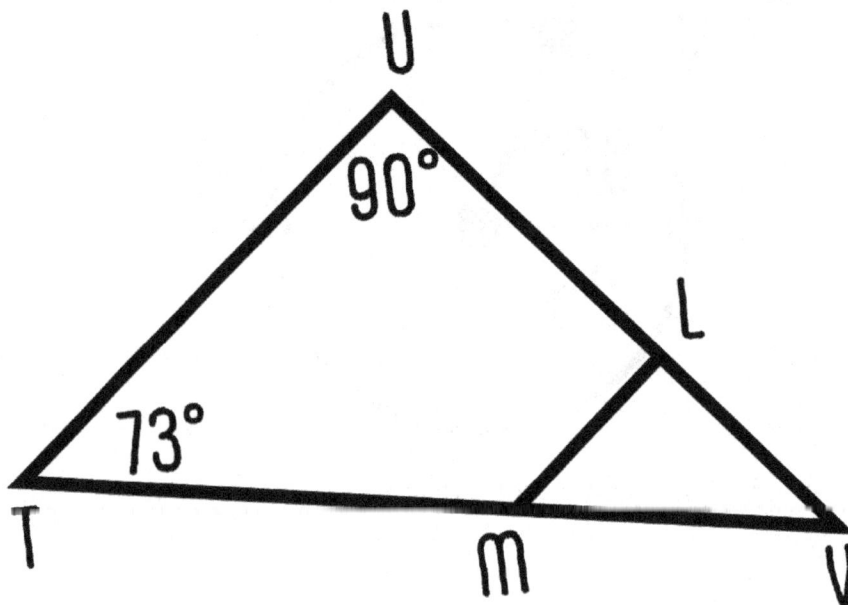

31. Write the converse of: "If Ana is wearing red, then she is at school."

32. Write the contrapositive of: "If Matthew is wearing boots, then he is at work."

33. Point G is Point F (-10, 8) translated by a vector of (3, 2). What are the coordinates of Point G?

34. A plank is leaning on the wall at an angle of elevation of 70°, The

plank is 6 feet long. How high does the plank reach on the wall

rounded to the nearest whole number?

35. Triangle JKL has one side measuring 3 inches. Triangle RST is

Triangle JKL dilated by a scale factor of 8. What is the length of the

corresponding side in Triangle RST?

36. A regular polygon's exterior angles each have a measure of 60°.

How many sides does the polygon have?

37. Rotate the figure below 180°.

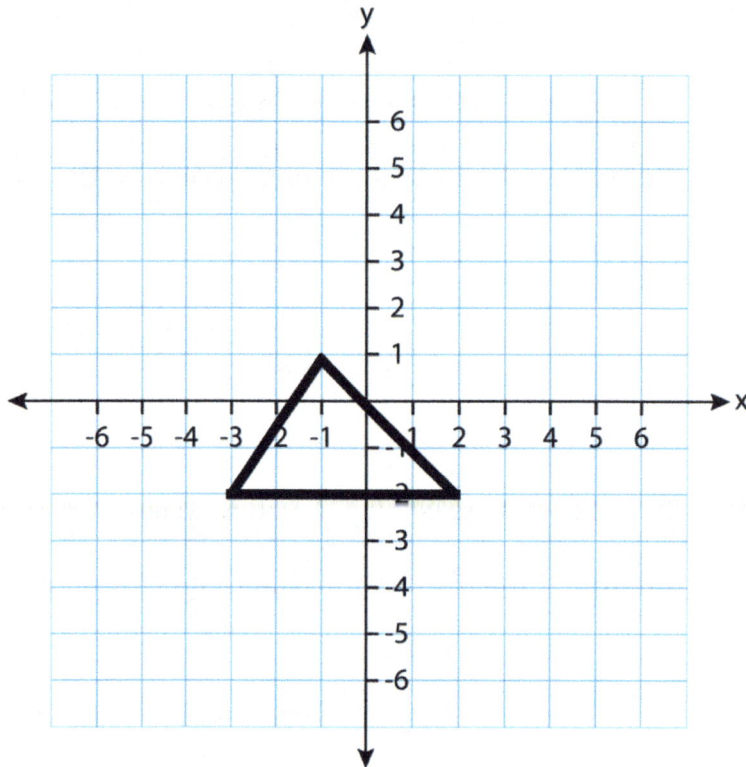

38. Triangle RST has vertices R (0, 7), S (-3, 1), and T (3, 1). What type of triangle is RST?

39. A circle has center (-5, 10) and radius 6. What is the equation of the circle?

40. Rotate the figure below 90° counterclockwise.

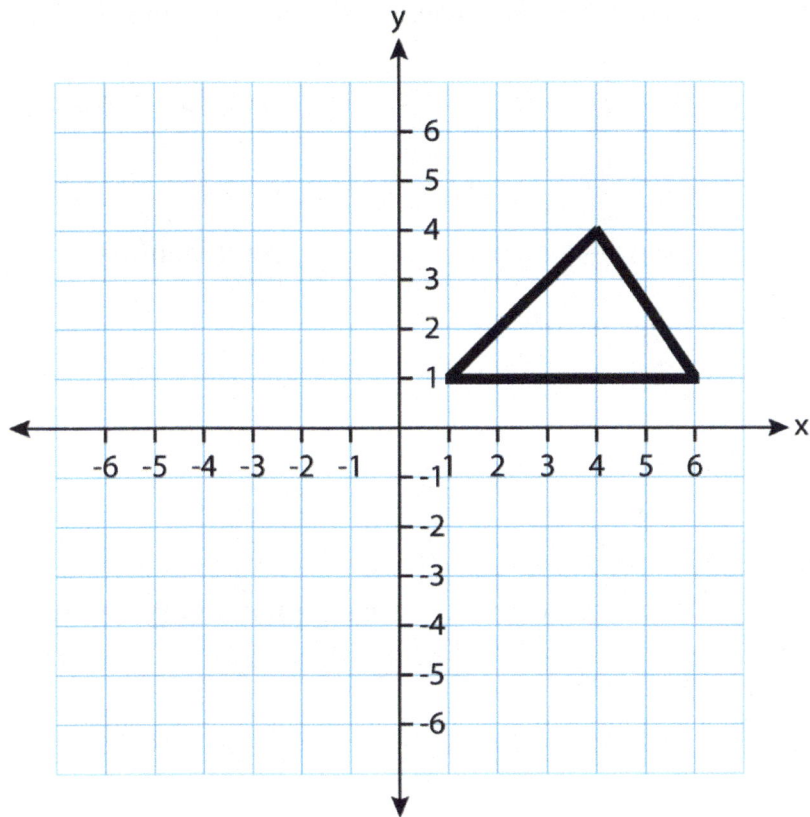

41. Rotate point C (9, 18) 90° counterclockwise around the origin.

42. A right triangle has side lengths 6 and 8. What is the length of the other side?

43. What is the slope of a line that is perpendicular to $10x - 2y = -6$

44. $\angle Y = 1x + 13$ and $\angle Z = 9x + 27$. $\angle Y$ and $\angle Z$ are complementary angles. What is the measure of $\angle Z$?

45. $\angle O = x + 13$ and $\angle C = x + 7$. $\angle O$ and $\angle C$ are supplementary angles. What is the measure of $\angle O$?

46. A line passes through the points $(9, 13)$ and $(3, 7)$. What is the slope of the line?

47. A polygon with 7 sides has angles 3x, 3x, 4x, 3x, 2x, 3x, and 2x.

   What is the value of x?

48. The interior angles of a polygon add up to 1440°. How many sides

   does the polygon have?

49. Angle B has a measure of 60 degrees. What is the measurement of

   x?

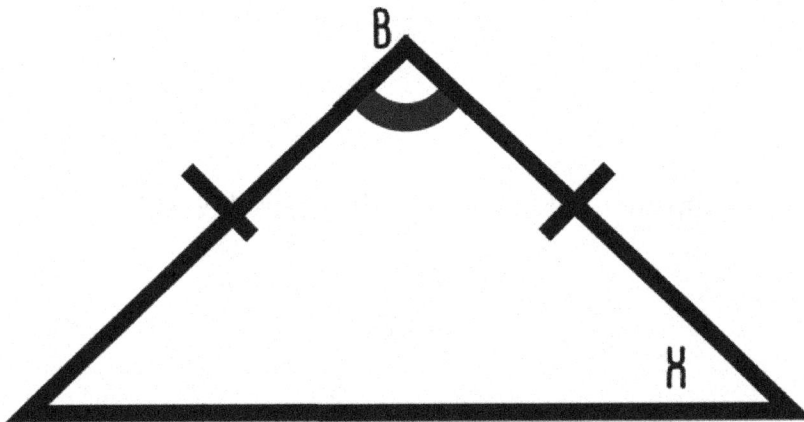

50. What is the slope of line QR?

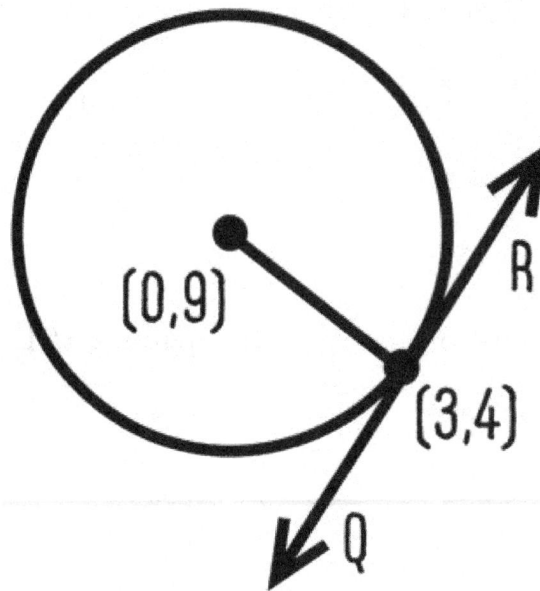

(0,9)

(3,4)

R

Q

51. What is the volume of a cube with side length 5 after the cube is

dilated by a scale factor of 3?

52. What is the measurement of angle M in the figure below?

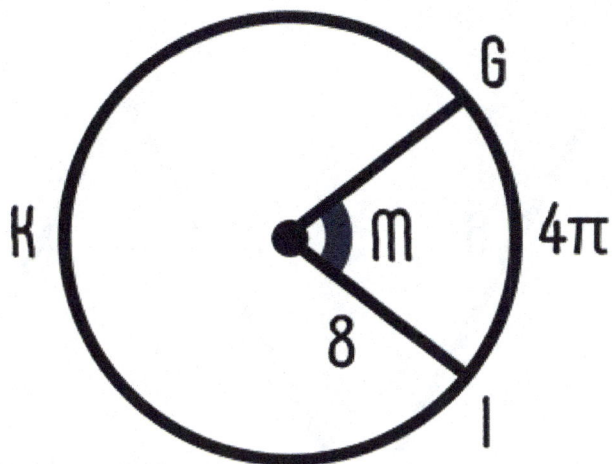

53. Reflect the figure below over the y-axis.

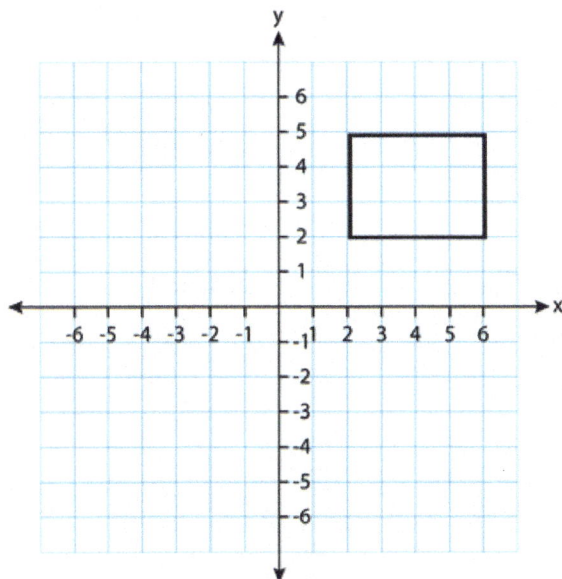

54. Are all the corresponding angles in the triangle below congruent?

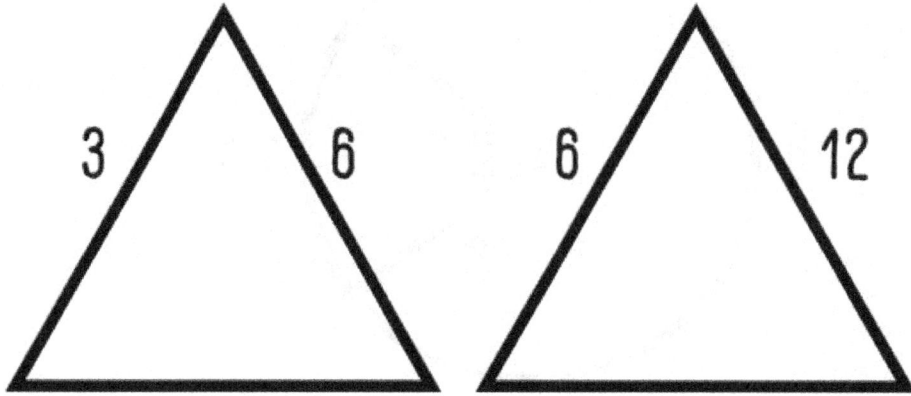

55. The interior angles of a polygon add up to 700 degrees. How many sides does the polygon have?

56. A circle has a diameter of 18. What is the circle's volume?

57. What is the area of a trapezoid with a base of 9 and 15 and a height of 6?

58. A nonagon has angle measures x, 2x, 3x, x, 2x, x, 2x, x, and x. What

   is the value of x?

59. Given: : ∠3 and ∠4 form a linear pair, and ∠3 = ∠4

   Prove: ∠3 and ∠4 are right angles

   Linear pairs add up to _____, so ∠3 + ∠4 = _____.

   Since they are congruent:

   $$\frac{180°}{2} \rightarrow \underline{\hspace{2cm}}$$

   ∠3 = _____

   ∠4 = _____

60. Cone A has a radius of 60 inches and a height of 30 inches. Cone B has a radius of 70 inches and a height of 40 inches. What is the difference between the volume of Cone B and Cone A?

61. A cube has volume $1,331\ feet^3$. What is the surface area of the cube?

62. The angles shown below are acute and complementary. N = 8x + 33. H = 4x + 69. What is the value of x?

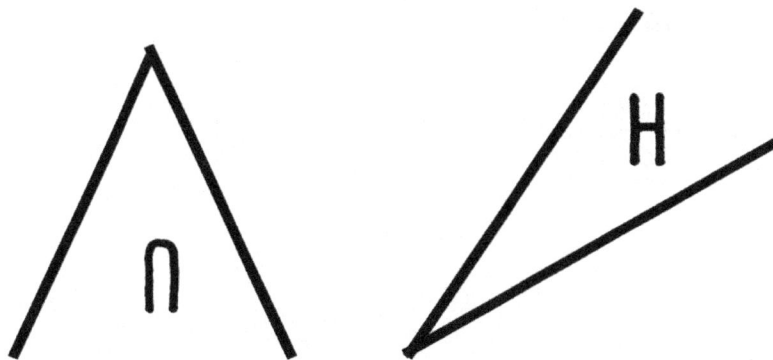

63. A triangle has points (4, 1), (-1, -3), and (4, -3). What is the slope of the triangle's hypotenuse?

64. What is the area of the figure below?

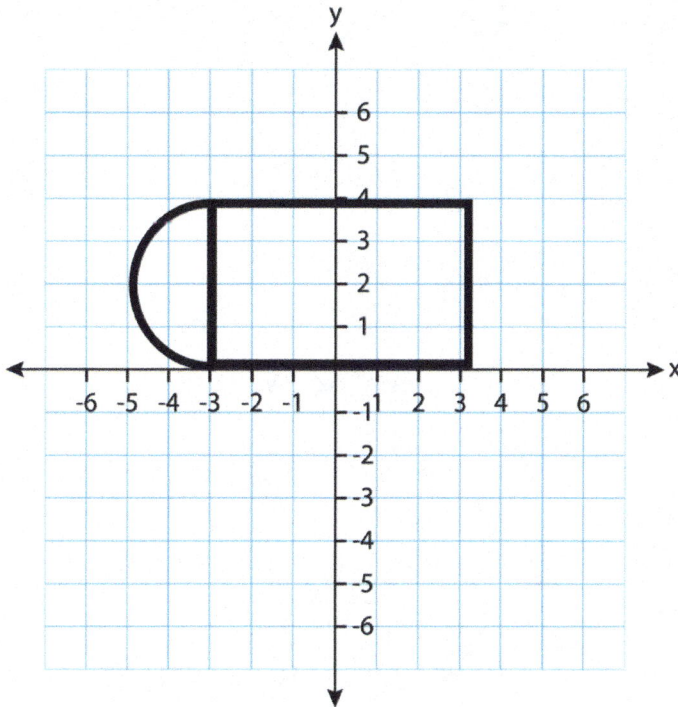

65. Reflect the figure below over the x -axis then rotate it 180.

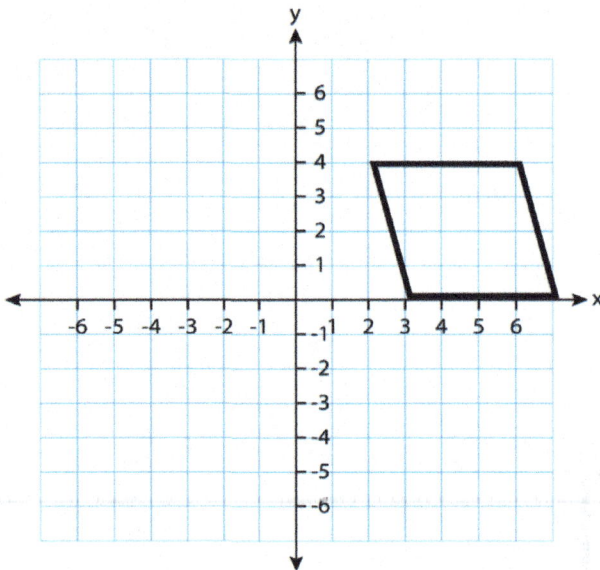

66. A triangle has a height of 16 and an area of 64. What is the triangle's base?

67. A pyramid has a base area of 8. Its volume is 216. What is the pyramid's height?

68. A triangle has a hypotenuse of 13 and a side length of 12. What is the other side's length?

69. ∠M and ∠N are supplementary angles. ∠M has a measurement of

23x – 12, and ∠N has a measurement of 17x - 8. What is the

measurement of ∠M?

70. ∠Q and ∠S are vertical angles. ∠Q has a measure of 8x + 24, and ∠S

has a measure of 12x – 8. What is the measure of ∠Q?

71. What is the surface area of a cube with a height of 7?

72. What is the diameter of a sphere that has a volume of 972π?

73. What is the exterior angle of a regular hexagon?

74. ∠W and ∠X form a linear pair. ∠W has a measurement of 18x – 26,

and ∠X has a measurement of 12x - 4. What is the value of x?

75. A semicircle has a radius of 4 feet. What is the length of its perimeter?

76. A circle has a circumference of 6π. What is its radius?

77. A triangle has angles measuring (4x − 20), (2x + 30), and (2x + 50). What is the value of x?

78. A square pyramid has a height of 3 and a base side length of 2. What is the volume?

79. A cylinder and cone have the same height and radius. The volume of the cylinder is $30in^3$. What is the volume of the cone?

80. A triangle has side lengths of 13, 12, and 5. Is this a right triangle?

81.Point K is Point J (9, 2) is rotated 90° clockwise centered around the origin. What are the coordinates of Point K?

82. A regular pentagon is inscribed in a circle. What is the measure of the angle formed at the center after connecting two adjacent vertices?

83. A square has a perimeter of 144. What is the diagonal length?

84. A cylinder has a diameter of 10 centimeters and a height of 14 centimeters. What is the cylinder's surface area rounded to the nearest whole number?

85. If Angle O and Angle K are both complimentary and congruent, then what is the measure of Angle 0?

86. A rectangle has side lengths 3x and 3x, and its area is 144. What is the value of x?

87. What is the equation of the line that goes between the points (3, 8) and (-5, 3)?

88. ∠J and ∠H are vertical angles. ∠J has a measure of 8x - 10 and ∠H has a measure of 6x. What is the measure of ∠H?

89. Can 5, 6, and 10 represent the side lengths of a right triangle?

90. Does the below statement use inductive or deductive reasoning? All mammals are warm blooded. All dogs are mammals. Dogs are warm blooded

91. ∠Y and ∠L are vertical angles. ∠Y has a measure of 78°. What is the measure of ∠L?

92. A cylinder and cone have the same base and height. Which figure has the greater volume?

93. What is the surface area of a cube with a volume of 27 $feet^3$?

94. A figure has triangle faces and a square base. What is the name of this figure?

95. What is the measure of the interior angle of a regular pentagon?

96. The volume of a cone is 96π cubic feet. If the height is 12 feet, then what is the radius rounded to the nearest whole number?

97. A circle fits perfectly inside a square. The square has an area of 36. What is the area, rounded to the nearest whole number, of the circle?

98. An equilateral triangle is inscribed in a circle. What is the measure of the angle formed at the center after connecting two adjacent vertices?

99. A circle is inscribed in a square. The square has an area of 49. What is the radius of the circle?

100. A circle is inscribed in a square. The square has an area of 4. What is the difference between the area of the square and the circle, rounded to the nearest hundredth?

101. ∠A in Triangle ABC measures 60°. ∠B and ∠C are congruent. What is the measure of ∠B?

102. A regular polygon has an interior angle sum of 1620°. How many sides does the polygon have?

103. Triangle EFG has EF and EG congruent. ∠F has a measure of 80°. What is the measure of ∠E?

104. ∠K and ∠L are complementary. ∠K is 17 times ∠L. What is the measure of ∠L?

105. Write the converse of: "If Sarah is wearing yellow, then it is July."

Geometry Crash Course   By Francesca Tamano

Answer Sheet

1. 34°. All the angles in a triangle add up to 180°. Thus, $180 - 84 - 62$

   $= 34$.

2. (28, -7). The midpoint formula is $\left(\frac{x_1 + x_2}{2}, \frac{y_1 + y_2}{2}\right)$. The midpoint is (7,

   4) and the endpoint is (-14, 15).

   a. $\frac{-14 + x}{2} = 7$. $-14 + x = 14$. Thus, $x = 28$.

   b. $\frac{15 + y}{2} = 4$. $15 + y = 8$. Thus, $y = -7$.

3. 60°. Parallel lines cut by a transversal have congruent

   corresponding angles.

4. 70°. Parallel lines cut by a transversal have congruent alternate

   exterior angles.

5. 42°. Supplementary angles add up to 180°.

6. 120°. The sum of angles in an n-gon is 180(n - 2), where n is the

   number of sides in the polygon. The polygon had 6 sides. Thus,

   180(6 - 2) = 720. Then, divide 720 by the number of angles. 720 / 6

   = 120.

7. 25. $7^2 + 24^2 = 625$. $\sqrt{625} = 2$

8. (0, -1/2). The midpoint formula is $\left(\frac{x_1 + x_2}{2}, \frac{y_1 + y_2}{2}\right)$. $\left(\frac{-4 + 4}{2}, \frac{3, -4}{2}\right) = (0, -$

   1/2)

9. Isosceles triangle. 2 sides are congruent.

10. About 44. The distance formula is $\sqrt{(x_2 - x_1)^2 + (y_2 - y_1)^2}$

11. Thus,

$$\sqrt{(36 - 9)^2 + (32 - 12)^2} = \sqrt{1129}$$

$$\sqrt{1129} \approx 44$$

12. 1407 cm². The formula for the surface area of a cylinder is

$2\pi h + 2\pi r^2 h.\ 2\pi(20) + 2\pi(8^2)(20) \approx 1407$.

13. (4, 8) and 4. The circle equation is $(x - h)^2 + (y - k)^2 = r^2$.

Regrouping $x^2 - 8x + y^2 - 16y = -64$ results in $(x^2 - 8x) +$

$(y^2 - 16y) = -64$. Now, we can complete the square for the x and

y terms. $\left(-\frac{8}{2}\right)^2 = 16.\ \left(-\frac{16}{2}\right)^2 = 64$. Then, $(x^2 - 8x + 16) +$

$(y^2 - 16y + 64) = -64 + 16 + 64$. Simplifying will result in

$(x - 4)^2 + (y - 8)^2 = 16$.

14. A circle circumscribed around a triangle includes all the triangle's

vertices.

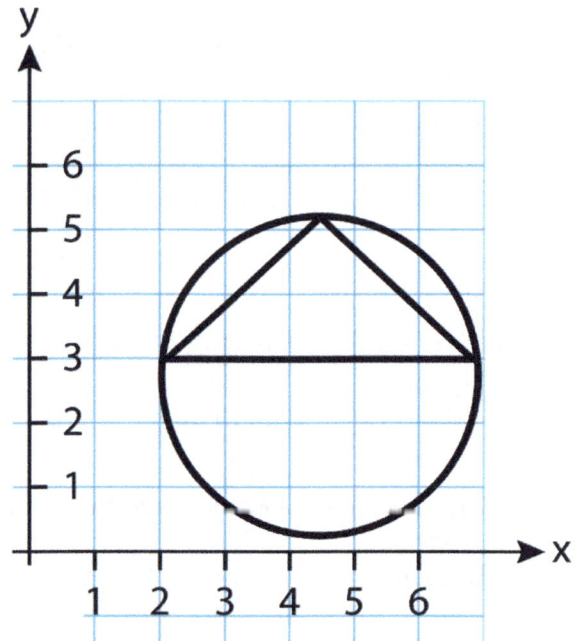

15. Density is mass / volume. $\frac{25}{3} \approx 8$.

16. 60/61. Cosine is adjacent / hypotenuse. The angle's adjacent side had a length of 60, and the hypotenuse had a length of 61.

17. Side Angle Side Theorem. The two triangles each have 2 congruent sides and a congruent angle between the sides.

18. Median. A median goes from the triangle's vertex to bisect the opposite segment.

19. If Bob is wearing his uniform, then Bob is at school. A converse reverses the conclusion and hypothesis. The original hypothesis was, "If Bob is at school," and the original conclusion was, "then Bob is wearing his uniform."

20. 120°.

21. Part A: 30. The length of the radius is 30. NH is the radius of the circle. A radius is a straight line extending from the center to the circumference of the circle. This is because N is the circle's center, and H is a point on the circle's circumference.

Part B: 50. The length of NM is 50. Segments NM, HM, and NH form a right triangle. HM and NH are both legs, and NM is the hypotenuse. Segment NH equals 30, and segment HM equals 40. $30^2 + 40^2 = 2500. \sqrt{2500} = 50$.

22. 283.5. The figures are a kite and a pentagon. The formula of a kite is $\frac{1}{2}d_1d_2$, where d_1 is the longest diagonal and d_2 is the other diagonal. The formula for the area of a pentagon is ½ P a, where P is the perimeter and a is the apothem. The area of the kite is $\left(\frac{1}{2}\right)(24)$ (18) = 216 The area of the pentagon is (1/2) (45) (3) = 67.5. 216 + 67.5 = 283.5.

23. $(x - 28)^2 + (y - 88)^2 = 80$. The circle equation is $(x - h)^2 + (y - k)^2 = r^2$, where (h, k) is the center and r is the radius. The two points given were (32, 80) and (24, 96). Since these points are the endpoints of the diameter, the midpoint between them is the center of the circle. The midpoint formula is

$\left(\dfrac{x_1 + x_2}{2}, \dfrac{y_1 + y_2}{2}\right)$. Thus, $\left(\dfrac{32 + 24}{2}, \dfrac{80 + 96}{2}\right) = (28, 88)$. Then, use

the distance formula to find the length of the radius.

$$\sqrt{(x_2 - x_1)^2 + (y_2 - y_1)^2} \cdot \sqrt{(28 - 32)^2 + (88 - 80)^2} = \sqrt{80}.$$

24. Part A: $(16, 13)$. $8 + 8 = 16$. $9 + 4 = 13$.

Part B: $4\sqrt{5}$. Point A is $(8, 9)$. Point W is $(16, 13)$. The distance

formula is $\sqrt{(x_2 - x_1)^2 + (y_2 - y_1)^2} \cdot \sqrt{(16 - 8)^2 + (13 - 9)^2}$

$= \sqrt{48}$. 16 is the largest perfect square factor of 48. $16 \cdot 4 = 48$.

25. $(x - 4)^2 + (y + 10)^2 = 126$. Complete the square for the equation

$x^2 + y^2 - 8x + 20y = 10$. $\left(-\dfrac{8}{2}\right)^2 = 16$. $x^2 + y^2 - 8x + 20y$

$+ 16 = 10 + 16$. $\left(\dfrac{20}{2}\right)^2 = 100$. $x^2 + y^2 - 8x + 20y$

$+ 16 + 100 = 10 + 16 + 100$. Simplify. $x^2 - 8x + 16 + y^2 + 20y$

$+ 100 = 126$. Factor to get $(x - 4)^2 + (y + 10)^2 = 126$.

26. $134\ cm^3$. The formula for volume of a cone is $\dfrac{1}{3}\pi r^2 h$. Rounded to

the nearest whole number, $\dfrac{1}{3}\pi (4)^2 (8) \approx 134$.

27. $871\ cm^3$. The formula for volume of a sphere is $\dfrac{4}{3}\pi r^3$. Thus, the

volume of Sphere A is $\dfrac{4}{3}\pi (6)^3$. The volume of Sphere B is $\dfrac{4}{3}\pi (2)^3$.

Rounded to the nearest whole number, the difference between the volumes of Sphere A and Sphere B is approximately 871 cm^3.

28. 131. The formula for circumference of a circle is $2\pi r$. 2 π (25) is the circle's circumference. 60/360 (2πr) is the length of arc XY. The length of XYZ is 300/360 (2πr). Thus, the length rounded to the nearest whole number is 131.

29. 1350 in^2. The formula for surface area of a cube is $6s^2$. The cube has an area of 3375 in^3. The formula for a cube's area is s^3. $\sqrt[3]{3375}$ = 15. The cube has side lengths of 15. 6 $(15)^2$ = 1350.

30. 6 ft. $\frac{1}{3} = \frac{x}{18}$. Cross multiply.

31. 73°. Similar triangles have congruent corresponding angles.

32. If Ana is at school, then she is wearing red. Hypothesis and conclusion are switched.

33. If Matthew is not at work, then he is not wearing boots. Hypothesis and conclusion are switched and negated.

34. (-7, 10). The vector values are added to the original values. The original point F = (-10, 8) and the vector = (3, 2). -10 + 3 = -7. 8 + 2 = 10.

35. 6 feet. Sin = opposite over hypotenuse. The hypotenuse is 6 feet. Sin (70°). = opposite / 6. Rounded to the nearest whole number, that results in about 6 feet.

36. 24 inches. $3(8) = 24$.

37. 6 sides. The number of sides in a polygon is (360° / one exterior angle's measure). $\frac{360}{60} = 60$.

38. The original points were (-1, 1), (-3, -2), and (2, -2). After a 180° rotation, the points will be (1, -1), (3, 2), and (-2, 2).

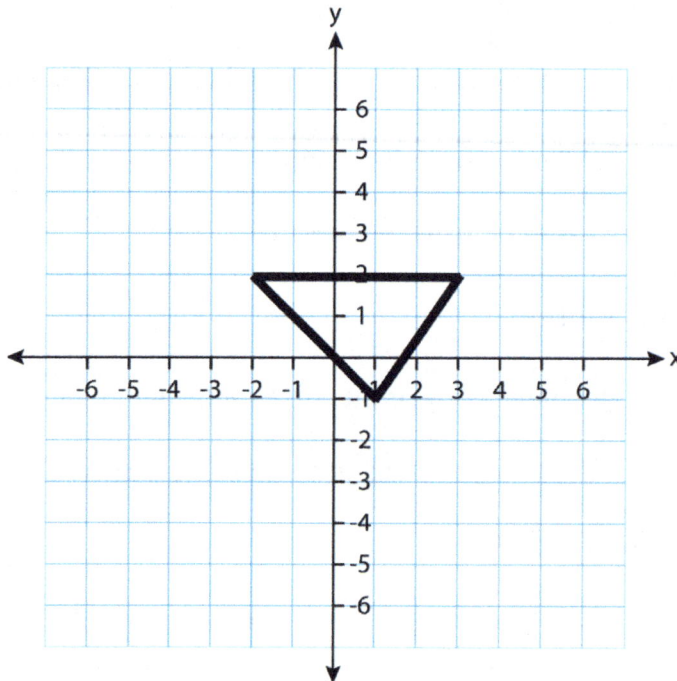

39. Isosceles triangle. The distance formula is

$$\sqrt{(x_2 - x_1)^2 + (y_2 - y_1)^2}$$. Side RS has a distance of

$\sqrt{(-3 - 0)^2 + (1 - 7)^2} = \sqrt{45}$. Side RT has a distance of

$\sqrt{(3 - 0)^2 + (1 - 7)^2} = \sqrt{45}$. Side ST has a distance of $\sqrt{(3{-}3)}$.

40. $(x + 5)^2 + (y - 10)^2 = 36$. The circle equation is

$$(x - h)^2 + (y - k)^2 = r^2$$, where (h, k) is the center and r is the

radius.

41. The original points were (1, 1), (6, 1), and (4, 4). After a 90°

counterclockwise rotation, the points will be (-1, 1), (-1, 6), and (-4,

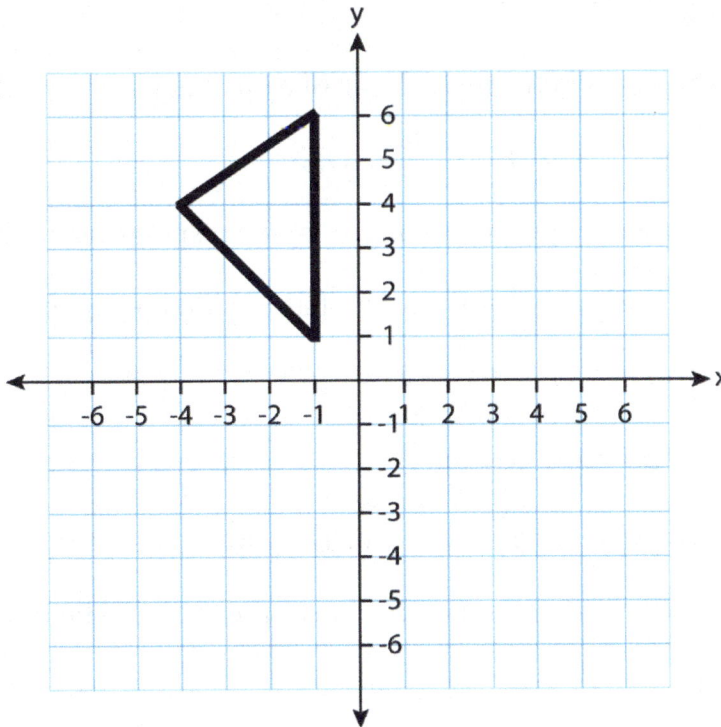

4).

42. (-18, 9). Under a 90° counterclockwise rotation, then point (x, y)

becomes (-y, x).

43. 10. The Pythagorean theorem is $a^2 + b^2 = c^2$. $6^2 + 8^2 = 100$.

$\sqrt{100} = 10$.

44. 72°. Complementary angles sum to 90°. Thus, (x + 13) + (9x + 27) = 90. x = 5. 9(5) + 27 = 72.

45. 60°. All angles in a triangle sum to 180°. 180 − 60 = 120. $\frac{120}{2} = 60$.

46. 3/5. Line QR is tangent to the circle. It is perpendicular to the radius. The radius has a slope of -5/3. The negative reciprocal of -5/3 is 3/5.

47. 3, 375. The formula for the volume of a cube is s^3. The cube was dilated by 3. 5 · 3 = 15. 15^3= 3, 375.

48. Yes. All similar shapes have congruent corresponding

49. 10 sides. The formula for the sum of an n-sided polygon's interior angles is 180 (n - 2). 180 (n - 2) = 1440.

50. 60°. 180 - 60 = 120. $\frac{120}{2} = 60$.

51. The slope of a line is rise over run. The radius has a slope of -5/3. The circle's tangent is perpendicular to the radius. The tangent has a slope of ⅗.

52. 3, 375. The formula for volume of a cube is s^3. The cube was dilated by 3. 5 · 3 = 15. 15^3= 3, 375.

53. 90°. The formula for circumference is $2\pi r$. $2(8)\pi = 16\pi$. The arc length is 4π. $\frac{x}{360} = \frac{4\pi}{16\pi}$.

54. A reflection over the y-axis is (x, y) $\rightarrow$ (-x, y).

Geometry Crash Course   By Francesca Tamano

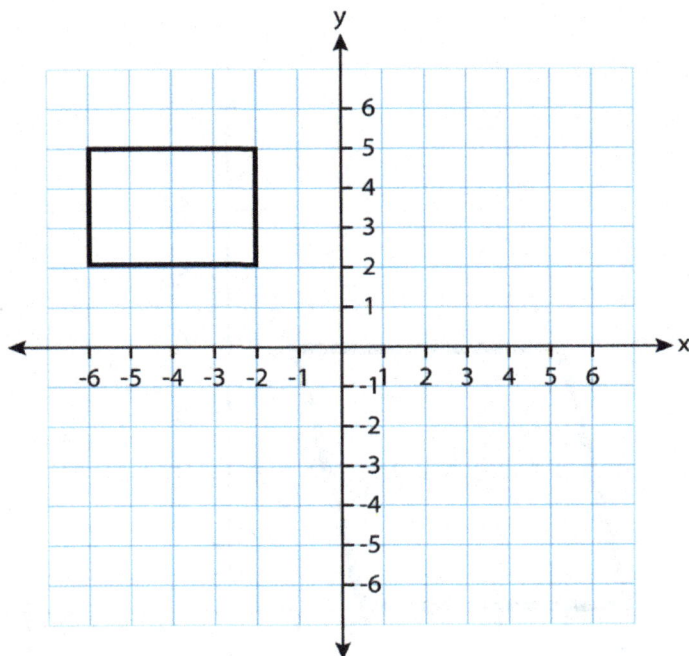

55.

56. 180 (n - 2) = 700. n = 53/9

57. 6. -8. x + 9 = -x - 7.

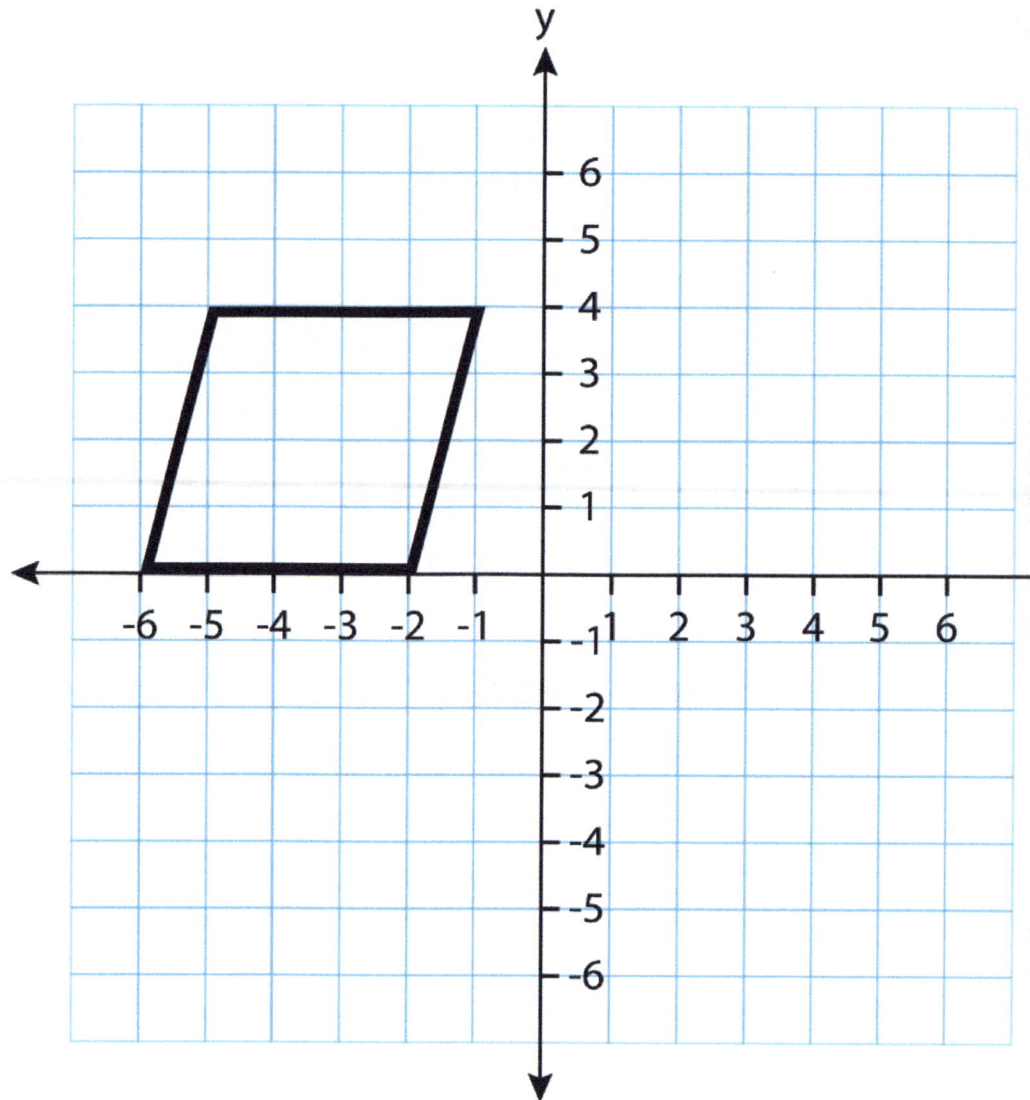

66. 8. The formula for the area of a triangle is ½ bh. 1/2b (16) = 64. b =

8

67. 81. The formula for a pyramid's volume is $\frac{1}{3}bh$. $\frac{8h}{3}$ = 216. h = 81

68.5. The Pythagorean theorem is $a^2 + b^2 = c^2$. $x^2 + 12^2 = 13^2$

. $x = 5$.

69. 103°. Supplementary angles sum to 180°. (

$23x - 12) + (17x - 8) = 180$. $x = 5$. $23(5) - 12 = 103$.

70. 88°. Vertical angles are congruent. $8x + 12 = 12x - 8$. $x = 8$. $8(8) +$

24 = 88.

71. 294. The formula for the surface area of a cube is $6x^2$, where x is the

side length. $6(7)^2 = 294$.

72. 18. The formula for volume of a sphere is $\frac{4}{3}\pi r^3$. is $\frac{4}{3}\pi r^3 = 972\pi$. R^3

$= 729$. R= 9. The formula for diameter is 2r. $9 \cdot 2 = 18$.

73. 60°. The formula for exterior angle of a regular hexagon is 360/6.

360/6= 60.

74. 7. A linear pair of angles has a sum of 180°. $(18x - 26) + (12x - 4) =$

180. x – 7.

75. 21 feet. The perimeter of the semicircle includes the diameter and

½ the circumference. The formula for diameter is 2r. Th formula

for circumference is $2\pi r$. Thus, rounded to the nearest whole

number, $2(4) + \pi(4)$, is about 21.

76. 3. The formula for circumference is $2\pi r$. $2\pi r = 6\pi$. r = 3.

77. 15. A triangle's interior angles sum to 180°. $(4x - 20) + (2x + 30) + (2x + 50) = 180$. $x = 15$.

78. 4. The formula for volume of a pyramid is $\frac{1}{3}bh$. The formula for area of a square is s^2. Thus, $\frac{1}{3}(2)^2(3) = 4$.

79. 10. The formula for volume of a cylinder is bh. The formula for volume of a cone is $\frac{1}{3}bh$. A cone's volume will be 1/3 the volume of a cylinder with congruent height and radius values. $\frac{1}{3} \cdot 30 = 10$.

80. Yes. The Pythagorean theorem is $a^2 + b^2 = c^2$. $5^2 + 12^2 = 13^2$.

81. (2, -9). Under a 90° clockwise rotation, then point (x, y) becomes (y, -x).

82. 72°. 120°. A circle is 360°. A regular pentagon inscribed within a circle divides the circle into 5 congruent arcs. 360/5 = 72.

83. If a circle is inscribed in a square, then what fraction of the square's area does the circle occupy?

84. 597 cm^2. The formula for surface area of a cylinder is $2\pi r^2 + 2\pi rh$. The diameter is 2r. 10/2 = 5. $2\pi(5)^2 + 2\pi(5)(14)$, rounded to the nearest whole number, is about 597.

85. 45°. Complementary angles sum to 90°. 2x = 90. x − 45.

86. 4. The formula for the area of a rectangle is lw. $3x^2 = 144$. x = 4.

87. $y = \frac{5}{8}x + \frac{49}{8}$. Slope is rise over run. $(3 - 8) = -5$. $(-5 - 3) = -8$.

The slope is $\frac{5}{8}x$. $y = \frac{5}{8}x + b$. Now, input one of the given points. $8 =$

$\frac{5}{8}(3) + b$. $b = \frac{49}{8}$.

88. 30°. Vertical angles are congruent. $8x - 10 = 6x$. $x = 5$. $6(5) = 30$.

89. No. The Pythagorean theorem is $a^2 + b^2 = c^2$. $5^2 + 6^2$ does

not equal 10^2.

90. Deductive reasoning. Deductive reasoning goes from the general to

the specific.

91. 78°. Vertical angles are congruent.

92. Cylinder. The formula for volume of a cylinder is bh. The formula

for volume of a cone is 1/3bh. The cylinder has three times the

volume of the cone with the same base and height.

93. 54. The formula for volume of a cube is s^3. $s^3 = 27$. $s = 3$. The

formula for surface area of a cube is $6s^2$. $6(9) = 54$.

94. Square pyramid.

95. 108°. The formula for the interior angle sum of an n-sided polygon

is 180(n-2). A pentagon has 5 sides. 180(5 - 2) = 540. 540/5 = 108.

96. 5 feet. The formula for volume of a cone is $\frac{1}{3}\pi r^2 h$. $.96\pi = \frac{1}{3}\pi r^2(12)$

. $r = \sqrt{24}$. r, rounded to the nearest whole number, is 5.

97. 28. The formula for the area of a square is s^2. $\sqrt{36} = 6$. The square has a side length of 6. The diameter of a circle is 6. The diameter is 2r. 6/2 = 3. The area of a circle is πr^2. $\pi (3)^2$, rounded to the nearest whole number, is about 28.

98. 120°. A circle is 360°. An equilateral triangle inscribed within a circle divides the circle into 3 congruent arcs. 360/3 = 120.

99. 3.5. The formula for area of a square is s^2. $\sqrt{49} = 7$. The square has a side length of 7. The diameter of a circle is 7. The diameter is 2r. 7/2 = 3.5.

100.   0.86. The formula for area of a square is s^2. The square has a side length of 2. Thus, the circle has a diameter of 2. The diameter is 2r. The circle has a radius of 1. The area of a circle is πr^2. The area of the circle is π. 4 - π is about, rounded to the nearest hundredth, 0.86.

101. 60°. The interior angles of a triangle sum to 180°. $\frac{(180-60)}{2} = 60$.

102. 11 sides. The formula for the interior angle sum of an n-sided polygon is 180(n - 2). $180(n - 2) = 1620$. n = 11.

103. 20°. Triangle EFG is an isosceles triangle. In an isosceles triangle, the base angles are congruent. The interior angles of a triangle sum to 180°. $180 - (80)(2) = 20$.

104. 5°. Complementary angles add up to 90°. x + 17x = 90. x = 5.

58. 105. If it is July, then Sarah is wearing yellow. A converse reverses

the conclusion and hypothesis. The original hypothesis was, "If

Sarah is wearing yellow," and the original conclusion was, "then it is

July."

Made in United States
Orlando, FL
12 June 2025